L E A N
R O B O T I C S

A Guide to Making Robots Work
in Your Factory

Samuel Bouchard

LEAN
ROBOTICS

A GUIDE TO MAKING
ROBOTS WORK IN
YOUR FACTORY

This book is for the makers.

It is dedicated to those who improve our lives with the stuff they make.

ACKNOWLEDGEMENTS

There are many people without whom this book would not have been possible.

First, I'd like to thank editor Kate Stern, who never shied away from challenging my ideas, and helped me greatly in refining the book's writing and structure.

My friend and long-term collaborator, graphic designer Jérémy Couture, was—as always—a master of grasping concepts and turning them into useful illustrations.

I'm enormously grateful to my friends and colleagues at Robotiq, our partners, and our customers from around the world. An especially big thank you goes to everyone who contributed to making this book better—you know who you are.

Finally, I wish to thank my family: Anick, Ellie, Chloé, Albert and Léo. It may have taken just a few months to get this book down on paper, but it took nine years to develop its content—nine years during which I have often been away from home. Thank you for all your support.

TABLE OF CONTENTS

LIST OF FIGURES

LIST OF TABLES

WHY I WROTE THIS BOOK

It was winter 2009, and I was on a mission to sell my startup's first product, a robotic gripper, to the automotive manufacturers of Michigan.

My cofounders and I—three friends from the robotics lab at Laval University—had a straightforward business plan for our new company, Robotiq.

At the time, every robotic gripper had custom-made fingers, so whenever manufacturers wanted to use grippers in their robotics-based assembly lines, they had to go through lots of trial and error regarding custom design and fabrication.

Our gripper, by contrast, was an off-the-shelf solution. With three articulated fingers that automatically adjusted to the object, it was able to grip practically any shape.

It also had 10 years of research and development behind it, and its robustness was proven in real-world nuclear site clean-up applications.

So if automotive manufacturers—the biggest consumers of robots—had any sense, they'd be lining up to buy it... right?

I drove to dozens of factories that winter to meet with the designers and assemblers of their robotic systems, who are called system integrators.

At each meeting, the system integrators would let me in, watch me demo the gripper, and respond with words to the effect of "thanks, but no thanks." Then I'd be politely shown the exit.

Sometimes they'd say the gripper seemed like cool technology—it was just too complicated, too expensive, and too inapplicable to any of their current projects.

After six months of non-stop effort, I had made precisely zero sales. I remember leaving the last meeting feeling utterly miserable. There was freezing rain on the roads of Michigan while I drove to the airport in my compact rental car with slick summer tires, hands clenching the wheel, trying to make it safely back home.

My thoughts went in circles: "What's wrong with our product? What did we miss? Am I just not trying hard enough?" One image came to mind: a trapped housefly butting against a windowpane, its persistence futile.

Sure, it was just after the crash of 2008. Few businesses were open to new ideas, since most of them were busy just trying to stay solvent. But was that the only reason we couldn't sell a single gripper?

I left Detroit on a flight back to Québec City, dwelling on the same anxious thoughts. Then I started to chat with the man sitting next to me. It so happened that he worked for one of the largest robotics system integrators in Detroit.

So as soon as he asked what I did, I pulled out my phone and showed him a video of our gripper—and he said "Why don't you come by in two weeks? That looks like it'd useful for one of my customer's projects." Finally, I felt our luck was beginning to turn.

When my team and I actually got to the man's facility, however, reality hit again. Our gripper—rather than being a time-saving solution like we'd advertised—ended up requiring three engineers to work for three full days just to connect it with the robot.

It was at that point that I finally realized two things. First, automotive manufacturers were right not to buy our product, because it didn't solve the problem of customized grippers. Second, that problem was a tiny one compared to the bigger issue: robotic system integration was way too costly and complicated!

We were working day and night on a company that was headed right into a wall. We had a product no one wanted to buy, and we were trying to solve an unimportant problem. How could we have missed these two vital pieces of information for so long?!

In my quest to answer this question, I came across a book on product development called *The Four Steps to the Epiphany* by Steve Blank. The book presents a method called customer development, which is a deliberate contrast to "product development." Blank argues that companies don't fail because they don't have any products, but because they don't have any customers. This was exactly the case for us. I had to keep reading.

Blank provides a step-by-step method to get the information you need from customers so you can develop products they will want to buy. At first, there are many unknowns: Who are our customers? What is their biggest problem? Who decides what to buy? How much are they willing to pay for it? Who would they buy it from? The list goes on.

Designing the right product requires a deep and complex understanding of the customers, the market, and the technology you can use to build the product. There are no perfectly defined answers. Yet, Blank managed to take a big, confusing problem and break it down in a way that even newbie entrepreneurs like me could follow.

We've been applying his methodology to all our subsequent products to make sure they'd have customers. Most of the time, it worked. When it failed, we'd always look back and realize there were places we did not apply the process properly. Eventually, it became second nature to follow the step-by-step process.

As for our realization that the biggest problem is "robotic system integration is too costly and complex," we worked to address parts of it with each of our subsequent products. This book is another step towards solving it.

Robotic cell deployment, like product development, is a process you can approach from many angles.

It often starts with broad, 'fuzzy' questions:

> *Can robots help my business? Can a robot do this task? Where should we put it? How do we set it up? Which technology should we choose? And where do we start?*

These are all questions you may have asked, only to hear "it depends" in response to every single one. It's true: the answers depend on the application, on your team's robotics skills, on your business objectives, and much more. That's because in manufacturing, the only thing that never changes from one factory to another... is that every factory is different!

But while there may never be a "one size fits all" robotic solution that can be used in every factory, I believe every factory can use a standard process. By implementing a clear, standardized, step-by-step methodology, we can break the fuzzy large-scale problem down into a series of smaller, more manageable pieces. We can be more successful at deploying robots that will drive our businesses forward.

That's why I wrote this book: to present the methodology my team and I have developed over the past nine years since Robotiq was founded.

The methodology is called lean robotics, and its goal **is to simplify the deployment of robots in factories.**

Lean robotics is based on our experience in supporting thousands of manufacturers worldwide, many of them first-time robot users, while they successfully deployed robots.

I sincerely hope you'll find it useful.

WHO THIS BOOK IS FOR

This book is a hands-on guide for anyone who wants to deploy robots to build stuff. Read on, and you'll learn how to design, integrate, and operate robots on your manufacturing floor as efficiently as possible.

Whether you're in charge of running a production operation or installing and maintaining production equipment, you'll find a step-by-step guide to making robots work in your factory.

If you're a manufacturing professional whose factory has already deployed robots, you'll be able to apply the concepts in this book right away. I'll show you methods you may not have considered, and point out ways to save time and money every time you work with robots in the future. You might be especially interested in the chapter on scaling up robotic cell deployment throughout your factory (or factories).

If you're a technology provider or system integrator in the robotics industry, you'll find fresh ways to look at the deployment process. These new approaches can help your collaborations with your manufacturing customers flow more smoothly.

> One assumption I make throughout this book is that you—the reader—work at a factory in the manufacturing industry.
>
> From now on, I'll often use the words "you," "manufacturer," and "factory" as synonyms. (This prevents me from having to say "assuming you want to deploy robots on a manufacturing factory floor..." before every piece of advice.)

Lean robotics, as you might have already guessed, is aligned with the lean manufacturing methodology (more on that soon). I've tried to avoid lean manufacturing jargon as much as possible; but just in case, you can find a glossary of lean manufacturing and lean robotics terms at the end of the book.

Most importantly, this book is designed to be self-contained. You don't need to be an expert in lean manufacturing to use the lean robotics methodology.

HOW ROBOTICS CELLS ARE DEPLOYED TODAY

Robots come in many forms; but from now on, I'll be using the word "robot" to refer to the robot arms—also known as industrial robots—used for manufacturing tasks.

What is a robot, anyway? If you're a manufacturer who wants robots to work in your factory, then you can think of a robot as an "automatically controlled... manipulator" (to paraphrase the International Federation of Robotics' definition, which is more detailed).[1]

However, there's not much you can do with just a robotic arm. You need other components too, which I'll describe below. That's why it makes more sense to talk about a **robotic cell** rather than just a robot.

In general, a cell is any station in the manufacturing process, such as on a production line, where a specific operation is being done. If the operation is done by a human, the station is known as a **manual cell** (see Fig. 1).

When factories install a robotic cell, their purpose is to automate a process. That process could be one that's currently done at a manual cell, or it could be an entirely new function.

As you may have guessed by now, a robotic cell is simply a station that includes a robot (Fig. 1).

---

(1) "An industrial robot is defined to be an 'automatically controlled, reprogrammable, multi-purpose manipulator, programmable in three or more axes, which can be either fixed in place or mobile for use in industrial automation applications.' " Source: "International robot standardization within ISO," IFR, https://ifr.org/standardisation.

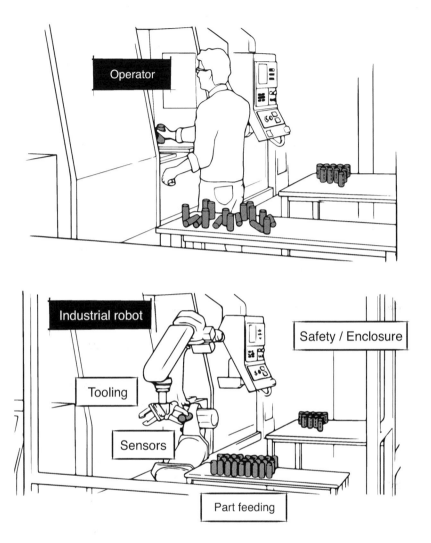

Fig. 1: Global view of a manual and a robotic cell.

When you buy a robotic arm, it comes with two important things: the **controller**, which is the computer that drives its movement, and the **teach pendant**, which is the user interface that the operator uses to program the robot. These are shown in Fig. 2.

If you think of the controller as a conventional desktop tower, the teach pendant would be your monitor and keyboard.

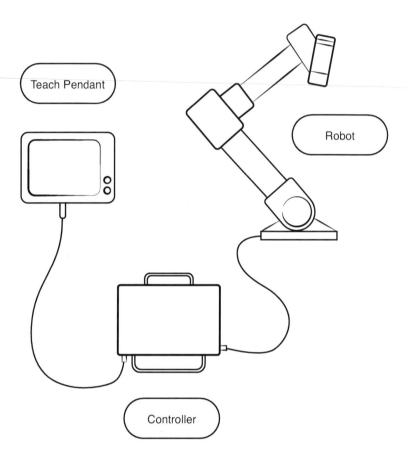

Fig. 2: Setup of industrial robot arm, controller, and teach pendant.

What comes after the robot's wrist, and what's added around the robot, varies depending on the application. But no matter the application, your robot will always need to be equipped with other components in order to work properly (Fig. 2).

These components might include **end-of-arm tools** (grippers, welding torches, polishing head, etc.) and **sensors** (such as force-torque sensors, safety sensors, vision systems, etc.).

You'll need to install the robot on your manufacturing floor by bolting it to a sturdy surface. Installation might also involve adding **part-feeding mechanisms, safeguards** like protective fencing, and more.

The robotic cell doesn't only include hardware. The controller comes with some pre-installed **software**, but you will have to write the **program**: the list of instructions the robot will follow to perform a specific task.

HOW DO YOU GET A ROBOTIC CELL TO WORK?

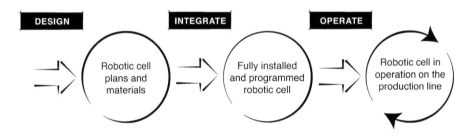

Fig. 3: Overview of the robotic cell deployment process.

Fig. 3 shows the main steps of the **robotic cell deployment process**: design, integrate, and operate.

1. The **design** phase includes all the tasks needed to go from the manual (or original) process to having the plan and materials for the robotic cell.
2. From there, the **integrate** phase consists of putting the pieces of the robotic cell together, programming it, and installing the cell on the production line.

3. The **operate** phase represents the end goal of deployment: having a productive robotic cell that does its job properly on an ongoing basis.

WHO PROVIDES WHAT?

When you buy a "robot" from a robotics company, you're typically only getting the arm, controller and teach pendant. Most robot companies do offer other hardware and software add-ons, but these don't cover every possible application.

That's why a whole industry has sprung up around providing application-specific solutions—and it's why the industrial robotics ecosystem is structured as shown in Fig. 4.

Different companies specialize in providing various pieces of the solution. Whoever does the cell deployment needs to put these solutions together themselves during the design and integrate phases.

The first two phases—design and integrate—can be done by an in-house team working for the manufacturer that has bought the robot, or by external contractors called **system integrators**. Of course, the buyer of the robot is responsible for operating it, so the third phase—operate—is done by the factory's team.

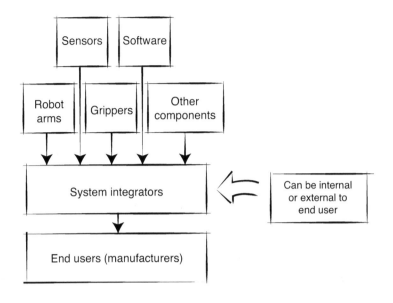

Fig. 4: Fragmentation of vendors in the industrial robotics industry.

ROBOTIC CELL DEPLOYMENT VS. ROBOTIC SYSTEM INTEGRATION

Throughout the book, we'll be using the phrase "robotic cell deploy-ment." You might be more familiar with the similar-sounding term "robotic system integration." But although these two phrases may seem similar, they actually have slightly different meanings.

ROBOTIC CELL VS. ROBOTIC SYSTEM

Lean robotics looks at a basic unit of production—a cell—that has a defined input, a process done by one operator, and an output.

A robotic system, on the other hand, *can* be a simple robotic cell, but it can also be much more complicated. It can include multiple robots, such as a production line station with 20 robots welding a car body simultaneously. Lean robotics is not the right tool for that kind of large, complex robotic system. It is a great fit, though, for a stand-alone cell with a single robot.

CELL DEPLOYMENT VS. SYSTEM INTEGRATION

Cell deployment includes the whole design-integrate-operate process, from defining the manual task to operating the robotic cell on the factory floor. By contrast, system integration typically covers the design and integrate phases only, and does not include the operate phase.

In lean robotics, we include the operate phase for a simple reason: the point of all of your work is to have the robot create value in the operate phase! So it's important to include it in order to see how the other two phases contribute to this end goal.

WHAT'S WRONG WITH HOW ROBOTIC CELLS ARE DEPLOYED TODAY?

Even today, with all the powerful robotics technology available and the number of important problems it can solve, the majority of manufacturing tasks are not yet automated.

THE MAIN BARRIER TO ROBOTIC CELL DEPLOYMENT IS HIGH COST

For a typical project involving a single robot, you may have to pay US$80,000 for a standard robot and its components. Then a system integrator will add another US$170,000 for other materials and custom engineering. In total, a turnkey solution ends up costing around US$250,000.

At that price, the predicted return on investment (ROI) might not be high enough to justify the cost of automating a manual task.

The reason it's so expensive is the complexity of robotic cell design and integration. Because of this complexity, a lot of costly project management, custom engineering, and specialized programming must be done. This is where the majority of the cost lies.

HERE ARE FOUR REASONS WHY ROBOTIC CELL DEPLOYMENT IS SO COMPLEX:

1. ROBOTS EVOLVED TO SUIT HIGH-VOLUME, LOW-MIX APPLICATIONS

The first reason is historical. Industrial robots were originally developed to serve automotive body manufacturers. Cars are produced in high volume, and because the products are so similar (low-mix) the same robot program can be used for several years. This means car manufacturers can amortize the cost of their custom system integration over the high number of cars made.

Moreover, in this context, reliability, speed and precision are more important than ease of use and simplicity of programming. Many robots on the market today were optimized with these constraints in mind.

But the constraints faced by the car makers of the past are not the same as those in many modern-day industries, where the time and money it takes to set up (or adapt) a robot can be much more important variables in the ROI calculation.

2. THERE IS A LACK OF STANDARDS IN THE ROBOTICS INDUSTRY

The second reason for complexity is the lack of standards across the highly fragmented robotics industry. Robotics standards are like toothbrushes: everyone agrees we should use them, but nobody wants to use someone else's.

As a result, each robot maker has its own unique controller and operating system. And they each support different communication protocols, which in many cases you must pay to use. No single vendor is dominant in the industry. So third-party developers who invest in one type of robot can only tap into a small fragment of the total market.

This is very different from an industry like smartphones, for example. If you build an application on a smartphone, you can use the display, microphone, camera, and GPS that are included with the operating system. Moreover, just two operating systems, iOS and Android, have captured the vast majority of the market. This has enabled a rich and diverse offering of applications from third-party developers.

In robotics, it's as if developers have to wire subsystems (equivalent to a phone's display, microphone, camera, etc.) together and get them to communicate using various communication protocols, before they can even start developing the app.

Thus, there is a lot of non-value-added work involved in robotics deployment. There's the technical challenge of integrating technologies that were never meant to work together, and the human-dynamics challenge of coordinating different vendors and project stakeholders, each of which may have various non-overlapping areas of expertise. And finally, all of this hard work results in products that can only be sold to a tiny fraction of the total robotics market.

What about ROS, the open-source robotic operating system platform developed by Willow Garage Inc.? In the book *Rise of the Robots: Technology and the Threat of a Jobless Future* (Basic Books, 2015), Martin Ford writes that "ROS is similar to operating systems like Microsoft Windows, Macintosh OS, or Google's Android, but is geared specifically toward making robots easy to program and control. Because ROS is free and also open source—meaning that software developers can easily modify and enhance it—it is rapidly becoming the standard software platform for robotics development" (from chapter 1, "The coming explosion in robotics," iBooks).

From this description, you might think ROS will soon provide a universal robotics standard. However, in reality it's far from being widely adopted in a broad variety of industrial applications. Instead, ROS is mostly used in research labs, because it was mainly designed to help developers build robots that work in unstructured environments. As such, ROS simplifies the work of PhDs who build outstanding adaptive machines, but it does not simplify the work of factory engineers who are automating semi-structured tasks.

Moreover, industrial robot manufacturers tend to stick to their own platforms for both commercial and technical reasons. Most importantly, their own platforms are far more robust than ROS. And on the commercial side of things, having their own platforms serves as a barrier to switching suppliers. System integrators typically invest a lot in training, so for integrators there's a high cost to switching to other robot vendors. These costs also mean that their customers at factories have an incentive to stick with the system they know.

3. ROBOTS DEAL WITH THE PHYSICAL WORLD

Unlike computers, which deal with digital information, robots must deal with the physical world as well. The information world is clean. It's made of bits, zeros and ones. The material world is messy. So even if robots had standardized hardware, communication protocols, and software, the fact is that the world around them can never be standardized.

Today's robots are good at following clear, repetitive and logical instructions. They're not as good at dealing with unstructured environments or improvising new methods.

The physics of the processes that the robot performs can also bring important deployment challenges. A typical example is welding. Reaching the right mix of part positioning, welding parameters and robot movement often means long hours of fine-tuning the robot's programming.

So long as robot programs must be customized to handle real-word objects, robot deployment will remain complex.

4. MANUFACTURERS LACK EMPLOYEES WHO ARE SKILLED IN ROBOTICS

One of the most common reasons why manufacturers don't use robots is that they lack employees with the robotics skills to manage them.

At many small and medium-sized enterprises (SMEs), there are no in-house robotics experts. A lack of internal skills doesn't just limit a company's capacity to take on a big robotics project; it can limit its ability to get started with just one robot.

Even if you think you have "in-house expertise," you might find you don't have as much of it as you would like. Factories might hire a few automation engineers with the idea that "robots" will be their responsibility, but those employees are often spread too thin, with too many other tasks to focus on robotic cell deployment.

Some multinationals have the same problem but at a different scale. When we work with large electronics contract manufacturers, for instance, they usually have robotics experts who can design sophisticated robotics solutions at the business's headquarters. The challenge arises when they have to install and operate the robots locally (on the factory floor).

With contract manufacturers, it's even harder to work around the lack of internal skills because production requirements can change quickly when a customer's product is far more or far less successful than predicted.

THE TRADEOFF BETWEEN COST AND DIFFICULTY

Manufacturers looking to deploy robotic cells today have two choices. They can delegate the project to an external system integrator or they can decide to do it themselves. Both are viable options, but they involve tradeoffs between cost and difficulty.

If you want to do it on your own, you can end up paying less, but you'll be dealing with complex aspects of deployment yourself. You might save time at first because unlike an external contractor, you're already thoroughly familiar with your current manufacturing processes.

However, you have to be realistic about your team's abilities. Even though your manufacturing and automation engineers are probably perfectly capable of learning how to use robots, consider how much they're capable of learning while carrying out the robotic cell deployment at the same time—in addition to taking care of all their other responsibilities within the factory.

A system integrator, on the other hand, will provide a turnkey solution at a fixed cost. You will benefit from the expertise they've accumulated from past projects. But this benefit must outweigh the inefficiencies introduced by their need to manage the project from outside your company and learn your manufacturing processes.

Every integration project has a certain amount of overhead costs, so system integrators might be reluctant to take on smaller projects. And if you have an integrator do the deployment for you, you'll remain somewhat dependent on the system integrator even after the robotic cell is installed (for maintenance, troubleshooting, etc.). All things considered, small projects might be both easier *and* more cost-effective for you to do by yourself.

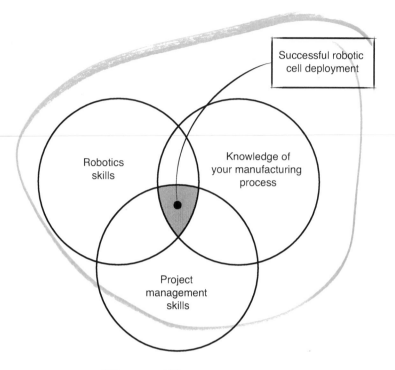

Fig. 5: Skills you need to successfully deploy a robotic cell.

To successfully deploy a robotic cell, you need team members with robotics skills, project management skills, and a deep knowledge of your manufacturing process (see Fig. 5).

The good news is you already have the most critical piece of the puzzle: knowing what your factory does that adds value for your customers.

The project management aspect is made easier when you use the lean robotics methodology. It clarifies the cell deployment steps and defines a common vocabulary, which will help you coordinate the project with different stakeholders.

Lean robotics will also help you pinpoint the technical robotics skills that your team needs to acquire for your specific business context.

Whether you choose to deploy the robotic cell on your own or with a system integrator, lean robotics will provide you with tools to make the process more efficient. A more efficient cell deployment project will be more cost-effective and provide a higher ROI.

By reducing some of the complexity of deployment, we're in turn removing part of the cost barrier, enabling you to automate more applications on your factory floor. This—as shown in Fig. 6—is the chain reaction that we want to create with lean robotics.

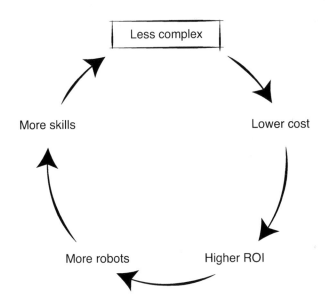

Fig. 6: The chain reaction of lean robotics.

37

A BETTER WAY: LEAN ROBOTICS

WHAT IS LEAN ROBOTICS?

Lean robotics is a method for efficiently deploying robotic cells in factories. The end goal—as with everything you do in your company—is to create value for your customers and drive business results.

Lean robotics isn't about technology *per se*, even though the methodology is applied via the technology of industrial robotics.

It consists of:

- Four core principles
- Three phases covering the robotic cell deployment process

These principles and phases are shown in Fig. 7.

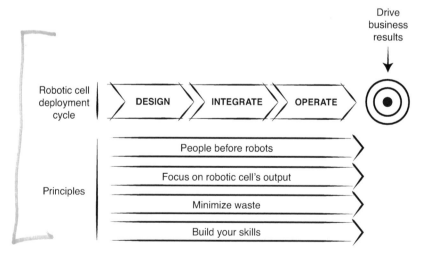

Fig. 7: Summary of the lean robotics methodology.

In the remainder of this book, I'll explain the principles and present a comprehensive guide to the deployment process. Along the way, you'll find in-depth examples, practical tools, and a section on business best practices that will help you succeed with lean robotics.

HOW LEAN ROBOTICS IS ALIGNED WITH LEAN MANUFACTURING

The lack of standards in robotics—of hardware, software, and technology in general—is hindering everyone's robotic cell deployment efforts. So the last thing I'd want to do is add yet another set of tools that might be incompatible with your existing ones! Lean robotics avoids this issue because it's well-aligned with lean manufacturing, a methodology that's common wisdom in the manufacturing industry.

As a manufacturing expert, chances are you're already familiar with many lean manufacturing concepts. Rather than start from scratch, I'll show you how to build on these concepts as you carry out your lean robotics projects.

Lean manufacturing is about:

1. **Customer value**—Defining value from the customer's point of view.
2. **Value creation chain**—Mapping the chain of activities that produce this value.
3. **Waste elimination**—Conserving resources and reducing waste along the chain.
4. **Continuous improvement**—Taking small yet steady steps towards perfection.

How do we apply all this to robotic cell deployment?

Robotic cells should not be treated any differently from the rest of the activities on your manufacturing floor. They are a means to an end: creating value for your customers. And as with lean manufacturing and agile programming, lean robotics is an iterative, bottom-up methodology.

With that in mind, we start by defining the customers and what they value:

1. **Customer value**—In a robotic cell, the "customer" is whatever step (or station) comes next on the production line. For this next station, "value" usually means receiving the right part, in the right way, at the right time, so the station can proceed with its operation.

2. **Value creation chain**—This can be different depending on what phase of the cell deployment you're in. In the operate phase, you want to look at the value-added transformation that the robotic cell executes on the parts it receives. In the design and integrate phases, the activities form a chain that will ultimately only generate value once the robotic cell is used for production.

3. **Waste elimination**—To maximize the return on your robotic cell investment, you must minimize waste. And you should do it throughout the entire robotic cell deployment cycle—that means at the design and integrate phases, not just during operation.

4. **Continuous improvement**—Lean robotics favors a robot-as-a-tool, bottom-up robotic cell deployment approach. It also encourages you to build your internal robotics and project management skills so you can keep continuously improving your robotic cell just like the rest of your production line.

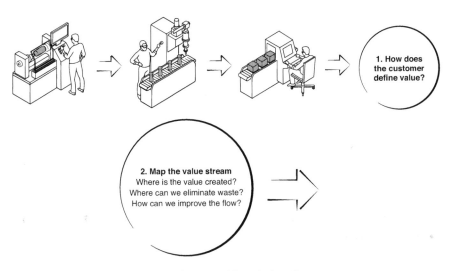

Fig. 8: The (simplified) lean manufacturing philosophy in action.

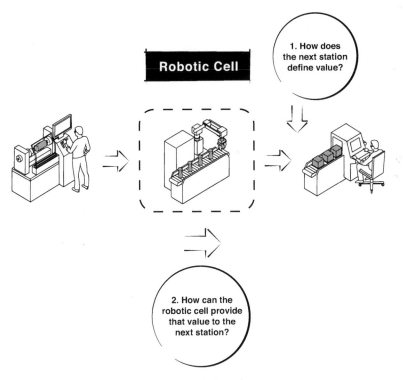

Fig. 9: The (simplified) lean robotics philosophy in action.

By comparing Fig. 8 with Fig. 9, you can see how the lean robotics approach is aligned with that of lean manufacturing.

Waste reduction is another important way in which the two approaches are aligned. Even though a big chunk of this book focuses on how to deploy a single robotic cell (with the design, integrate, and operate phases), the "lean" waste reduction aspect really comes into play when you're scaling up your efforts and deploying multiple cells.

Everyone knows it's important for newly-installed robots to be productive once they're up and running. But what many robotics users often don't realize is that productivity is just as important during the design and integrate phases.

Today, these first two phases involve a tremendous amount of waste. You have to spend time communicating what the project's about to your team members, waiting for equipment to arrive, debugging your programs, re-engineering things that someone has certainly done before...

We tend not to question whether all this is necessary because it seems like creative, problem-solving engineering work. But that's where we're wrong! All this waste leads to a hugely negative impact for your company, because these two phases have a tremendous leverage effect in both the short and long terms. Each step of the design and integrate phases should be about creating value for the customer while reducing as much waste as possible.

When you have a robotic deployment project done on time, and done correctly the first time, as opposed to one that's completed three months behind schedule, you have an additional three months' worth of automated production. Plus, when you structure your work so that components of your first project can be reused in your next one, you can reduce your deployment time and increase the ROI. In practice, I've seen manufacturers obtain a 50% shorter deployment time and

50% higher ROI in their second cell deployment project, simply by following lean robotics practices with the first cell deployment.

HOW ROBOTS CAN AFFECT YOUR LEAN MANUFACTURING EFFORTS

In the attempt to make factories more "lean," robots can be both a help and a hindrance.

Sometimes robots can introduce new sources of waste that might actually work against your lean manufacturing efforts, such as in the following cases:

- A robotic cell that requires new non-value-added tasks to be done.
    - For example, if parts arrive at the robotic cell in unstructured packaging that the robot cannot handle, a human operator might have to manually place the parts in a mechanical fixture so the robot can pick them. The creation of the fixture and the operator's work are both non-value-added activities that were not part of the process before the robot was introduced.

- A robotic cell **monument** (see glossary) that reduces your factory's flexibility.
    - A typical example of a monument is the massive robotic cell in a car factory that pairs the chassis with the car's body. In order to work, these so-called "marriage cells" require two separate production lines (one for the chassis, one for the body) to converge at a specific point in space and time. All other materials must flow in alignment with this cell, so it's difficult to change the factory's layout when improvements need to be made.

However, these costs are often outweighed by the many benefits robots can bring to your lean manufacturing efforts, such as:

- Improvement of product quality.
  - › Because robots are excellent at doing the exact same operation again and again, they have the potential to improve your production line's consistency and reduce the number of defective products.
- Elimination of human ergonomic constraints on the production line.
  - › Sometimes the production line's capacity is constrained by human limitations, such as when manual operators simply cannot go any faster. If that's what's slowing down production, robots can increase your output.
- Time savings.
  - › Even if robots don't reduce production time directly, it's better to have a robot standing idle than a human employee or a multimillion-dollar machine.
- Prevention of human health and safety issues.
  - › For example, one factory was able to eliminate workers' carpal tunnel problems by having a robot take over the tasks that were causing them.
- Renewed focus on waste reduction practices.
  - › When you use robots, you're forced to sort through the work process and standardize tasks and parts. You also have to ensure the parts are delivered to the robot in a consistent manner, and that they're ready for the robot to work on. In doing so, you'll automatically apply lean manufacturing waste reduction practices by eliminating some non-value-added tasks (such as part preparation, cleaning, etc. by manual operators).
- Automatic **error-proofing** (see glossary).
  - › For example, let's say you have two parts of different sizes being presented to the robot. The robot gripper needs to be able to recognize when it's presented with the wrong part, so you could add a mechanical or software solution for doing so.
  - › Similarly, the robot can signal when something's gone wrong at the station (making use of the lean concept **andon,** see glossary). The robot can go into a specific visible position or cause a light to flash, letting human operators know they need to take action.

- Avoidance of wasted human potential.
  - › Humans can create much more value in your factory when they're working creatively rather than repeating the exact same motions day after day. Robots can take care of this necessary yet low-value-added work instead; and workers can take on higher-impact tasks.

Clearly, the amount of waste that may be added or removed is just one aspect of lean manufacturing. So you might not care about additional waste induced by robots if they can help your factory achieve other goals, such as increasing output, improving quality, or shipping products on time.

That's why it's up to you to evaluate the pros and cons of robots with respect to your factory's unique context—in terms of both your lean manufacturing efforts and your business's overall goals.

PRINCIPLES OF LEAN ROBOTICS

The four principles presented in this section will help you make sound decisions throughout the entire deployment sequence.

1. PEOPLE BEFORE ROBOTS

Isaac Asimov, a brilliant science fiction writer and professor of biochemistry, famously came up with the "Three Laws of Robotics":

1. A robot may not injure a human being or, through inaction, allow a human being to come to harm.
2. A robot must obey the orders given it by human beings except where such orders would conflict with the First Law.
3. A robot must protect its own existence as long as such protection does not conflict with the First or Second Laws.

Modern artificial intelligence is not as advanced as in Asimov's stories. Until it is, these rules must be administered and followed by those of us who deploy and program robots, rather than by the robots themselves.

With that in mind, a simple way to summarize the Three Laws is with the principle of *people before robots*.

This principle has two components:

A. Robotic cells must be safe for humans.

B. Robots must be tools usable by all.

These are the guidelines that we, and all members of the robotics community, must abide by if we are to make robots work for us.

A. ROBOTIC CELLS MUST BE SAFE FOR HUMANS

Worker safety is a core aspect of our society's values and legal regulations (or at least it's intended to be), and we must strive to uphold it. Like everything else in your factory, robots should not harm humans.

So, how do you make sure your new machine will be safe for everyone around it? The process usually follows these steps:

1. Evaluate the risk.
2. Mitigate the sources of risk until they reach an acceptably low level (in terms of the combined likelihood of occurrence and expected severity).

This process is called a risk assessment. Just as you would when adding any new machine, a risk assessment should be performed while planning the deployment of a robotic cell.

Your risk assessment must be done in accordance with the following:

- Corporate safety rules and guidelines.
- Local regulations on workers' safety.
- Guidelines published by the ISO (International Standard for Organization) and/or a country-specific equivalent.

The ISO publishes several standards regarding the safety of robotic systems and collaborative robots. While these standards are only guidelines, they're often used as the basis for the law, so it's worth becoming familiar with them.

Need help with safety issues? Here are some resources:

- External robotic system integrators
- Robotics industry associations, many of which offer training in robotic safety
- Machinery safety experts who are proficient in robotic risk assessment

The bottom line is that robots must serve humans; obviously, the last thing they should do is hurt them!

Keep in mind that robots can also improve workers' safety. For example, one company, a furniture manufacturer, now uses a robot to feed sheet metal into a punch press. Before introducing the robot, a human operator was exposed to the dangers of sharp parts and the punch press.

B. ROBOTS MUST BE TOOLS USABLE BY ALL

This means we should aim to make robotic cells that are accessible and understandable by everyone. From a lean manufacturing stand-point, there are two main benefits.

First, if robots can be used and adapted by all your workers, it will create great synergy in your business: humans can identify areas for improvements, and robots can follow their instructions.

When workers gain robotics expertise, they'll start looking for more opportunities to use robots to improve productivity, ergonomics, output quality, etc. In this way, you'll be implementing the "continuous improvement" aspect of lean manufacturing on the factory floor. So even if workers can't deploy the robots themselves on day one, they'll soon be able to contribute by identifying problems robots can solve.

It's of great strategic importance that you start building that expertise today. If you do, then over time your team's skill level will increase while robotic technologies become easier to use. By narrowing the skills gap from both of these angles, you'll have more people ready to deploy robots as quickly as possible—ideally much sooner than your competitors.

Second, implementing this principle is also a way to avoid the risk of having too few people who understand how to use the robot(s).

For example, I once met an owner of a small metal job shop who had trouble hiring enough welders to fill his orders, so he decided to invest in his first robotic cell. He programmed the robot himself and operated it to great success. But when other aspects of his business began demanding more of his attention, he no longer had time to run the robot.

He wasn't able to find a robot programmer he could hire to replace him, and he couldn't program new additions to the robot himself. Eventually he was forced to transition his shop back to manual welding, because even though it was hard to find welders, they were still easier to find than robot programmers.

Imagine if the robot was simple enough to become another one of the welder's tools—if instead of needing one programmer (who knows nothing about welding) to teach the robot, the shop owner could have had one welder teaching 10 robots? Then the welder's value-creating knowledge could be leveraged across multiple robotic cells.

WHAT DOES IT TAKE TO HAVE ROBOTS BECOME TOOLS AVAILABLE TO ALL WORKERS?

Your priority is to choose robot technologies that can do the jobs they're intended for, while being operable by as many people as possible in your factory. That could mean choosing robots that are controlled by the most user-friendly interfaces or the simplest programming commands, so you can train more workers to use them.

As new technologies become available, it will become easier for more people to use them, since user-interfaces are constantly being updated. However, in the meantime your organization will still have to work to ensure its employees can use them.

Even if you can't achieve "robots as tools for all" from day one, you'll find it worthwhile to at least have several people able to operate, maintain, and improve your robotic cells. That way, your robotic workforce will be more adaptable to your business needs, and your key engineers will be able to focus on high-impact robotic projects rather than lower-level maintenance work.

A NOTE ON "PEOPLE BEFORE ROBOTS" AND THE FUTURE OF JOBS

"People before robots" might seem like an idealistic notion that can't (or won't) be applied in reality, especially if you listen to what mainstream media outlets have to say on the topic.

It seems not a day goes by without a new article popping up on my Twitter feed, blaring something along the lines of "Robots are stealing your jobs."[1] So I can see why some might question how people can be more important than robots, if robots will end up taking over people's jobs.

In response to these concerns, the robotics industry often likes to get out their PR team and launch a counter-attack, attempting to explain why in fact robots are creating a net increase in jobs.[2]

But I think both parties are missing the point.

The robotics industry's usual argument is that companies and countries that use robots create more jobs. However, the most innovative

---

(1) For example, see this political cartoon in U.S. News featuring an employment centre staffed by robots: https://www.usnews.com/cartoons/economy-cartoons?int=opinion-rec.

(2) For example, see this article on the International Federation of Robotics website: "Robots create jobs!," https://ifr.org/robots-create-jobs.

companies also use more robots—and obviously, more innovative companies are likely to do better financially, and hence create more jobs.

Since innovative companies are more successful, and the use of robots can indicate innovation in manufacturing, that could be where this trend is coming from. Perhaps robots are not necessarily *causing* the job creation; they might simply be correlated with it.

On the other hand, it seems the media have got it backwards. Rather than worrying about robots stealing our jobs in 20 years, we should be worrying about the number of jobs going undone right now because manufacturers can't find people to do them!

For the most part, manufacturers aren't bringing in robots to replace people—they're bringing in robots because they don't have *enough* people.

This phenomenon—of being unable to find enough human workers to fill job openings—is known as the skills gap, and it's affecting manufacturers worldwide. Although the extent of the skills gap in other sectors of the economy is widely debated, a gap certainly exists in the manufacturing industries of countries such as the United States, Canada, and China.[3]

As Cait Murphy explains in an article for *Inc.*, "It is not so much that the U.S. has a skills gap [overall], but that *there are specific issues in specific places.*"[4]

I've seen this first-hand here in Canada, where one of Robotiq's customers is a machinery maker. The business cannot find enough workers to serve all its customers. Any employee they can bring

(3) Regarding China, see "The $250 billion question: Can China close the skills gap?," McKinsey & Co., June 25, 2013, http://mckinseychina.com/the-250-billion-question-can-china-close-the-skills-gap/.

(4) Cait Murphy, "Is There Really a Skills Gap?," Inc., April 2014, www.inc.com/magazine/201404/cait-murphy/skills-gap-in-the-labor-force.html

onboard has a direct impact on their revenue, because every additional employee means they can fulfill many more orders.

Another factory in the small town of Bromont, Québec, sends a shuttle to bring in workers from Montreal every day—a 185 km or 115 mile journey, round-trip—because too few of them are willing to move to Bromont permanently.

And as Murphy goes on to say in the same article:

> One of the areas in which there is undoubtedly a skills shortage now (and a bigger one looming) is welding; the average age of a welder is 55, and the country could be short as many as 291,000 of them by 2020, according to the American Welding Society.[5]

Moreover, deploying robots in factories doesn't mean getting rid of all workers, since humans will still be needed for creative work, strategic-thinking tasks, and operation of robots.

Some may agree that humans will still be needed in the short term, but object that in the long-run, machines are destined to become more intelligent than humans—and if that happens, even marketing teams and managers will likely find themselves replaced by robots.[6]

However, if machines become more intelligent than humans, lots of things will change. We don't know what will happen, exactly... and neither does anyone else. The best we can do is focus on what's within our control right now (see Fig. 10).

---

(5) Ibid.

(6) For example, Emanuel Marot argues "Very soon, robots will be replacing humans in top management positions, even up to the CEO level," in "Robot CEO: Your next boss could run on code," Venture Beat, March 20, 2016, https://venturebeat.com/2016/03/20/robot-ceo-your-next-boss-could-run-on-code/.

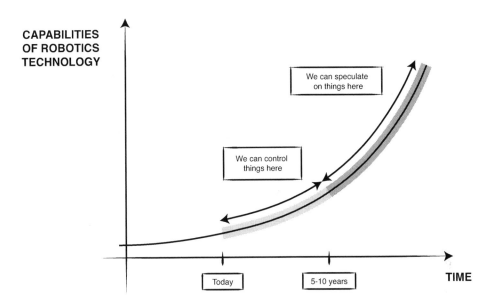

CAPABILITIES OF ROBOTICS TECHNOLOGY

We can speculate on things here

We can control things here

Today

5-10 years

TIME

Fig. 10: The exponential curve of progress in robotics technology.

The fact is that robots will inevitably be put to work in greater and greater numbers. There's no point arguing whether or not this is a good thing. Instead, we should focus on solutions and how we can make sure the shift towards robots in factories is done right.

At this point you might be wondering: if greater automation is inevitable, why should you bother reading this book? Well, just because something will happen eventually, doesn't mean you should sit idly by while the world changes around you. Whether you're a CEO, manager, factory worker, or student, you can start benefitting from robots today—and the rest of this book will show you how.

2. FOCUS ON THE ROBOTIC CELL'S OUTPUT

Your job as a manufacturer is to profit from making products that consumers are willing to pay for. This is why lean manufacturing is popular with so many companies: it helps the manufacturer focus on creating value for the consumer while eliminating waste along the way.

In lean manufacturing, the overall goal is to better serve whatever company or person is giving money to your business—the external customer. It's easy to define "value" from the external customer's perspective, since it's the reason why the consumer is willing to exchange cash or another form of payment for your product (or service).

To achieve the end goal of lean manufacturing, you sometimes have to focus on serving the *internal* customer first. The internal customer is the process, station, department, etc., that will receive a given output within the factory.

In lean robotics, the main focus is always on serving the internal customer, and it's defined as whatever station comes after the robotic cell in the production sequence. This "customer" obviously doesn't pay for things with currency—instead, it defines value as receiving the right parts, with the right presentation, at the right time, so it can in turn create value.

Keep in mind that in both lean manufacturing and lean robotics, an activity is considered value-added if it meets the following three criteria:

1. It must transform the product or service.
2. The customer must be willing to "pay" for it.
3. It must be done correctly the first time.

Accordingly, in the design and integrate phases you're adding value by creating a robotic cell that's ready to operate—the robotic cell itself is your "product." Anything that doesn't directly contribute to having a working robotic cell is non-value-added.

In the operate phase, the product is whatever the cell is delivering to the next station in the manufacturing process. And what's valuable for that next process is to receive the right parts, the right way, at the right time to be able to do its job.

Now, "non-value-added" doesn't mean "useless." Many non-value-added tasks, such as packaging, are still inherently necessary.

With packaging, for instance, the external customer is paying for the product, not the packaging, yet the product must be packaged in order to be shipped.

Since non-value-added tasks can still be necessary, it's possible for a robotic cell to provide value to its customer by doing a non-value-added task.

For example, your robotic cell could be a quality control station that checks whether the previous station output non-defective parts. The robotic cell's customer might be the shipping department, which values receiving non-defective parts. So this robotic cell provides value to its customer by identifying defective parts, even though this is not actually a "value-added" process.

A simple rule of thumb for robotic cells in the operate phase is that process-oriented tasks, such as welding, polishing, painting, and assembly, are typically value-added. By contrast, material handling tasks are typically non-value-added. These include machine loading/unloading, packaging, palletizing, inspection, and quality assurance.

To summarize, the principle of focusing on the robotic cell's output means the following:

- **The robotic cell must create value for its customer.**

    a. The robotic cell customer is the next station in the production sequence—the one that receives the robotic cell's output as an input.

    b. This customer defines value as receiving the right parts, with the right presentation, at the right time, so it can in turn create value.

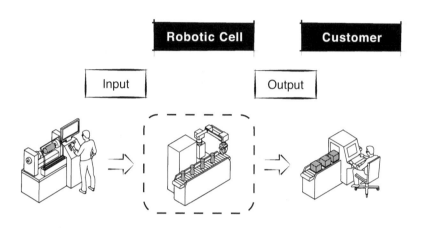

Fig. 11: Example of robotic cell delivering value to a customer.

In the design phase of deploying the robotic cell, you should start by answering this question: what is the value that the robot should be creating for the next station on the factory floor? If you fail to sort out how your robotic cell will create value for the next station, everything you do in the design and integration phases will be worthless. This puts the emphasis on delivering a reliable, working robotic cell the first time.

Another aspect of starting with the end in mind is targeting the simplest possible cell that will do the job. The lean robotics approach for the deployment of any robotic cell is to first target the minimum viable robotic cell.

Product development teams use the concept of minimum viable product.[7] The MVP is defined as a product with just enough features (and no more) to satisfy early customers, who will provide feedback for future development. This approach brings advantages in a highly dynamic environment, where information is gathered while the product is still evolving. The goal is to create, within the constraints of minimum cost and time, a product that the consumer is actually willing to pay for.

The minimum viable robotic cell (MVRC) is the robotic cell with just enough features (and no more) that can reliably create value for its customer.

Here's why the MVRC approach is the right way to go:

- The work done at the design and integration stages can only create value if the cell ends up working reliably in the operation stage. Adding complexity could diminish the value that can be created by the robotic cell, because it may delay the launch date and reduce reliability.

- Robotic cell design and integration almost always takes longer than expected. It's sometimes tempting to add features along the way, but you should stick with what you need and avoid the "nice to have's."

- The context in which your cell operates will probably change along the way. You can't possibly know all the relevant information at the beginning of the design stage—first because all the stakeholders will be learning throughout the deployment process (about robot possibilities, limitations, effects on other factors, etc.), and second because the company's environment—both physically and in the business sphere—might be changing rapidly. The more time it takes to deploy the robotic cell, the more likely it is that the context will have changed by the time it's operating. That's why the cell design should be kept flexible enough to remain open to future improvements.

- Your robotic cell will need to evolve to keep up with future developments, so you should view the robotic cell deployment project not as a final destination, but as another step in your lean manufacturing journey.

---

(7) For more on the MVP concept, see https://en.wikipedia.org/wiki/Minimum_viable_product.

- One last important aspect related to this principle is that you should measure how much value the robotic cell is producing for its customer (the next station). This will be the basis for your evaluation of whether the robotic cell is doing its job the way you had planned. It will also be a key metric to track while you aim for continuous improvement of the cell. I'll talk about this more later, but for now just keep in mind that you should start by focusing on customer value, which involves coming up with the minimum viable cell, and thinking about how you'll measure the value it creates.

3. MINIMIZE WASTE

Every time energy is transferred, some waste is inevitable. There is no known process in which 100% of the input is transformed directly into the desired output. Car motors can't convert all their fuel into movement, solar panels can't convert 100% of the solar energy they receive into electricity, and you don't obtain nutrients from 100% of the food you eat.

It's the same in a business. The various processes are never 100% efficient.

In lean manufacturing, waste is defined as energy and money that is spent but not converted into value for the customer. So for a business, waste is the difference between the energy and money we put into something, and the actual result that we get.

Lean manufacturing defines three broad categories of waste:

1. **Mura**—Waste due to variation.
2. **Muri**—Waste due to overstressing or overburdening people or equipment.
3. **Muda**—An activity that consumes resources without creating value for the customer.

Muda is typically broken down into seven specific types of waste:

1. **Transportation**—Non-value-added movement of parts, materials, or information—both within the factory, and between it and its partner institutions (other plants, suppliers, warehouses, etc.).
2. **Waiting**—When people, parts, systems, or facilities stand idly by while they wait for a work cycle to be completed.
3. **Overproduction**—Producing outputs more quickly, or in greater quantities, than customers demand.
4. **Defects**—Producing outputs so flawed that customers would deem them unacceptable.
5. **Inventory**—Accumulating leftover raw materials, works-in-progress (WIPs), or finished goods that will not contribute to value creation.
6. **Movement**—Unnecessary movement of workers, materials, or equipment during a single processing step or within a single station.
7. **Extra Processing**—Performing additional work, even though it is not required to meet the customer's standards.

There is an eighth type of muda—one that's not always defined in lean manufacturing, but is perhaps the most important type in lean robotics:

8. **Underutilizing Human Potential**[8]—When employees are capable of making greater contributions, yet prevented from doing so because of the other tasks they need to perform.

We'll discuss at various points in the book how lean robotics can impact the different types of waste and what to do about it. It's important to reduce waste throughout the entire cell deployment cycle.

---

(8) I prefer to use the word "potential" rather than "talent" when describing the eighth type of waste, because one's potential can be developed, whereas one's talent is typically thought of as innate or fixed. This idea comes from the book *Mindset: The New Psychology of Success* by Carol Dweck (Ballantine Books-Penguin Random House, 2016).

When deploying the robotic cell, we tend to focus on reducing waste at the operate stage, because that's the easiest place to do so. You know exactly what your inputs and outputs are, so it's easy to track them. But lean robotics is about optimizing the design and integration stages as well.

As a manufacturer, the production floor isn't the only area that should be concerned with productivity. It should also—and perhaps even more so—be at the forefront of your engineering teams' minds. Everyone knows waste must be eliminated on the factory floor, and it's easier to assign numbers to activities performed on the production line (like seconds, dollars, etc.), but remember: you should be paying just as much attention to the robotic deployment tasks performed by engineers and technicians, because they have an important leverage effect.

Let's say you deploy robots with an internal team and start a timer the day you receive the equipment. If the robotic cells can't start production until two months after they were supposed to, the point where you'll break even on your investment will be at least two months delayed, and possibly even more considering the extra costs incurred by those delays. If the challenge you want to solve with the robot is to increase capacity, then the cost is even higher: it's the lost chance to make use of the extra capacity that would have been provided by the robots over the two months, had they been working on schedule. Depending on what you're producing, the negative financial impact of delays can be significant.

Fig. 12 depicts two timelines: one showing the impact of non-value-added activities in a typical robotic cell deployment project like this one, and one showing the ideal scenario, where non-value-added activities have been eliminated.

This image illustrates the positive impact of reducing waste throughout the cell deployment cycle.

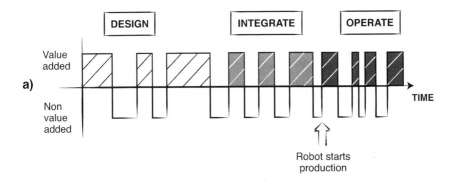

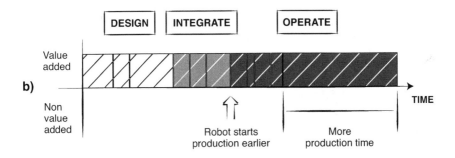

Fig. 12: Two cell deployment timelines: a) typical cell deployment with numerous non-value-added tasks; b) ideal cell deployment with no non-value-added tasks. Note how much earlier the cell enters production in the ideal timeline, and how much more uptime there is in this timeline's operate phase.

We can categorize waste in robotic cell deployment phases according to the eight types of lean manufacturing waste.

If you're a manufacturing engineer, the idea that you should avoid these types of waste in the operate phase is probably already clear to you. However, you should be paying just as much attention to waste in the design and integrate phases as well.

In the section on scaling up your robotic cell deployment, we'll cover several tools that will help you identify and reduce waste across robotic cell deployment projects.

4. LEVERAGE YOUR SKILLS

At this point you might be asking "Who cares about building 'internal' robotics skills? All I want to do with my robotic cell is set it and forget it. Can't I just subcontract it out to an external system integrator?"

Those "set and forget" robotic applications might sound compelling, but unfortunately they often won't align with the reality of your factory's needs. A factory floor is a dynamic place: new products are developed, existing ones are improved, capacity is adjusted up and down, new regulations are introduced, customer requests are handled… The set and forget applications, by contrast, are designed for a single purpose, so implementing them will limit the potential positive impact of robots in your factory. So you can see why deploying the robotic cell with your own team, using the bottom-up lean robotics approach, is a much more flexible option than outsourcing.

Imagine the benefits of leveraging your skills over time. If your factory could potentially make use of 10 robotic cells, and you're able to install each one quicker and less expensively than before, how much would this increase your return on investment? Some of our customers have deployed hundreds of robotic cells by themselves. As they progressed, their robotic cell deployments became easier, more reliable, more cost-effective, and quicker to generate value. The keys to this leverage effect are reusing the human skills (learning) and robot skills (technological building blocks) that are developed in early projects.

Of course, there's only so much you can improve. In manufacturing, the path towards perfection is asymptotic: you can gradually get better, but you'll never quite reach perfection. Plus, "perfection" is a moving target because the context is changing all the time. In lean robotics, there's no point trying to be completely perfect today: it's impossible and you'll only end up over-engineering your robotic cell.

What you should do is take small steps in the *direction* of perfection. So what does perfection mean here? What would be the perfect lean robotics implementation for your factory? To answer that question, you should take a holistic view of your enterprise:

- Evaluate the long-term potential of lean robotics for all your operations.
- Find the right balance of deployment costs vs. benefits, for the short-term vs. the long-term.

If you have a small shop with only one application that could use a robotic cell, your perspective on long-term lean robotics will be limited to this single application. In your situation, focus on first deploying the minimum viable robotic cell (MVRC). Once your MVRC has started generating value, evaluate how you can improve it to support your lean manufacturing efforts. But don't try to do it all at once. Keep in mind that you will learn important lessons and that your environment and technology will keep evolving. So delivering one working cell and *then* improving it will be smoother and more rewarding than trying to do everything simultaneously.

However, if you're like most of the manufacturers I've encountered in the last decade, your first robotic cell will not be your last. It may seem daunting at the start, but once you've overcome the challenge of installing your first cell, you'll already be looking for the next one. And you'll be well on your way to leveraging your skills.

Keeping the four core principles in mind, now let's see how to put them into practice in the lean robotics cell deployment cycle.

DEPLOYING YOUR ROBOTIC CELL

Let's start by looking at the complete robotic cell deployment cycle, as shown in Fig. 13.

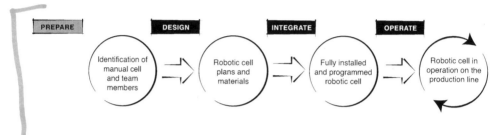

Fig. 13: Overview of phases in the lean robotics cell deployment sequence.

PREPARE

When you decide to deploy a robotic cell, it's usually because you're aiming to solve some issues in your company regarding productivity, quality, or output capacity.

In the project definition phase, you should identify the **scope of your project**. This includes:

- The specific **manual cell** you intend to automate.
- The **metrics** you want to improve.
- A **timeline** for the project.

Once these have been defined, the next steps are to assemble your team and communicate these goals before you officially launch the project.

ASSEMBLE THE TEAM

Who will be kept informed about the robotic cell deployment project? Who will be put in charge? And who will actually carry it out?

Table 1 lists all the roles people will play in a robotic cell deployment project. To keep track of who's responsible for what, you could add a column on the right and fill it in with the name of the relevant team member. A template is available on leanrobotics.org.

In larger organizations, people's roles might seem to be predefined by their job titles. However, several roles might still be played by the same person, as is often the case in smaller factories. I've even seen shop owner-operators do every single task by themselves.

Table 1: Roles and responsibilities involved in robotic cell deployment. *RACI*

Role	Objective	Responsibilities	Key performance indicators (KPIs)
Manufacturing manager	Align the project with the company's objectives.	• Provide project team with necessary resources • Exercise leadership to keep the team on track • Communicate news of the project to everyone in the factory	• All manufacturing KPIs that are affected by the robotic cell project
Project leader	Define the project's scope and requirements.	• Define which manual cell to automate and why • Define which metrics should be improved, the cell's target specifications, and the minimum viable cell • Monitor the cell's productivity once in operation	• Robotic cell's KPIs (when operating)

Role	Objective	Responsibilities	Key performance indicators (KPIs)
Project coordinator	Ensure the project is done on spec, on time, and on budget.	• Manage use of project resources • Facilitate communication between the project team and other teams in the factory • Schedule the different phases of integration	• Budget and expenses • Project schedule • Project targets [are met/are not met]
Engineer	Design a robotic cell that will meet requirements.	• Document the current manual process and constraints • Develop robotic cell concepts • Calculate ROI • Design the cell • List materials needed to build the cell and their cost • Test and prototype • Document final cell • Develop training material for operation and maintenance workers	• Requirements of robotic cell • Engineering schedule and budget
Installer	Assemble the robotic cell components together.	• Assemble the (initially) free-standing robotic cell • Perform mechanical and electrical installation • Install the robotic cell on the production line	• Cell is fully installed and ready for programming [yes/no] • Installation schedule and budget

Role	Objective	Responsibilities	Key performance indicators (KPIs)
Programmer	Program the robot to perform as intended.	• Program the robot • Ensure program meets standards for clarity and readability • Define levels of access to the robot's program (who can modify what) • Set up the interface between the robotic cell and other machines so they can communicate • Provide documentation for the program • Back up the system	• Performance and reliability of program • Programming schedule and budget
Operation and maintenance worker	Operate and maintain a productive robotic cell.	• Start the robot • Troubleshoot whenever the cell stops working • Keep a log of problems and solutions, and provide feedback to rest of team • Bring unresolved problems to the attention of robotic cell project leader • Carry out preventive and reactive maintenance tasks	• Productivity of robotic cell
Process advisor	Ensure the robotic cell process meets or exceeds quality standards.	• Advise the robotic cell designer and programmer on the process to be done at the cell	• Process quality measures
Procurement	Purchase the right equipment when needed.	• Purchase robotic cell equipment • Ensure purchases are received on time and stored properly	• The right equipment is received on time for the right price [yes/no]

Role	Objective	Responsibilities	Key performance indicators (KPIs)
Continuous improvement	Improve the robotic cell over time.	• Identify how the robotic cell and overall process could be improved • Coordinate continuous improvement projects	• All KPIs that are targeted for improvement

Sometimes the job title alone doesn't capture all the responsibilities of a role. In these cases, people might overlook some crucial tasks.

For instance, the manufacturing manager is responsible for communicating news about the project to everyone in the factory. This isn't about saying "We're installing a robotic cell. Deal with it." Managers have to define the project's *raison d'être*—the reason why robots will benefit everyone in the company—and ensure everyone understands it. (I'll go into more detail on how to do this in the next subsection.)

On another note, sometimes people underestimate the importance of certain roles, such as the project leader. Since deploying your first robot involves innovation and change, you need strong leadership—both technical *and* managerial.

Don't ignore the process advisor, either. It's easy to overlook small steps in the manual process, especially with value-added processes like assembly, welding, or polishing. Casual statements like "By the way, once in awhile I have to hammer this corner to get the jig in" or "Oh yeah, sometimes I manually remove the extra burr so I can assemble the two parts" might seem insignificant, but if the robotic cell isn't set up to do these tasks, the whole project could fail. That's why you need a process advisor who will pay close attention to everything your current operators have to say about their jobs. In fact, the operators of the current manual cell usually make the best process advisors.

Lastly, don't assign critical deployment tasks to people who are already 100% dedicated to other important projects in the factory. Be realistic about how many tasks each team member can take on. No matter how big or small your organization is, you might need to bring in new people.

EXPLAIN THE PROJECT

Manufacturing managers, this section is for you. One of your most important jobs is to explain what's happening with the robotic cell deployment in a way that's compelling yet free of bullshit.

If you don't tell people what's going on, they'll tend to assume the worst (whether in robotic cell deployment or life). And once these misperceptions spread, they're hard to get rid of. It's much easier to simply provide the right information in the first place.

Get your facts together and communicate your vision early and often—better to lean towards too much communication than too little.

START BY GATHERING THE INFORMATION

Once the project has been defined and team members selected, you should prepare a brief document or presentation that outlines the following:

- **Why**—Figure out why the company is investing in robotics before you discuss how you'll go about doing it. When people understand the "why," they'll be able to better contribute to the "how."[1]

---

[1] For more on this concept, see the book *Start with Why: How Great Leaders Inspire Everyone to Take Action* by Simon Sinek (Portfolio-Penguin, 2009).

- **Scope**—What is the cell (or activities in a cell) to be automated? Where does the cell start and end, in terms of the production process?
- **Schedule**—On what (target) date will the cell be up and running? How about the main steps in between—when will they be completed?
- **Roles**—Who will be assigned to each task? What is each person responsible for, exactly?

For the moment, the purpose of this document is just to help you keep track of important information. Later, you will present it at the project's announcement session.

NEXT, DEVELOP A STRATEGY FOR ANSWERING QUESTIONS

It helps to conduct a frequently-asked-questions brainstorming session with your management and HR teams before you announce the project. Do your best to predict all the questions people might have about the project, and have your answers ready.

Typical questions might be:

- Will I be safe around the robot?
- What will I do during the project?
- If the robot does this task, will there be anything left for me to do?
- Are you planning to lay off all the employees?

Consider the people who will probably be most concerned about the project, and figure out how you'll respond to their anxiety. You might be able to work with your HR department to support workers who might be negatively impacted by the introduction of robots.

Also, even if most people understand why their employer wants to make a change, they'll still be asking themselves "What's in it for me?" It's a fair question, and you should be proactive in answering it.

One great tool for answering questions is video case studies that show workers, engineers and managers discussing their previous concerns, how they accomplished the cell deployment, and what effect it had.

LAY THE GROUNDWORK WITH MOBILIZERS

Whenever a project is being "sold" internally, mobilizers are the people with the biggest influence on project dynamics.

Before kicking off the project, you might want to invest some time in meeting with your mobilizers as well as the workers you think could be most concerned about the changes the project will bring for them.

The goal here is to prevent yourself from hosting a meeting to announce the project where all your employees hear is "Robots are coming whether we like it or not."

ANNOUNCE THE PROJECT

At the kickoff session, you'll present the integration project as a mission to be accomplished. Gather everyone involved in the project, and explain what each person (or team) will work on and why it's important. You can start the meeting off in a conference room, but it's often a good idea to go to where the action will take place, namely the relevant station on the factory floor.

This is where you'll present that information you prepared earlier (in the "gather information" step).

Remember that your audience might not have the same background information as you, so avoid jargon, particularly when it comes to technical terms.

Of course, your job doesn't end here. You should keep people updated on the cell deployment's progress, and share what an impact it's had once the robotic cell is fully in production.

Effective communication at a remanufacturing facility

A remanufacturing facility in Mississippi decided to introduce robots for performing repetitive tasks. Dean, the engineer in charge of the project, started to engage with suppliers who came to look at their application and conduct robotic arm demonstrations on the factory floor. After a few meetings, Dean realized that employees had become concerned about robots and (untrue) rumors of layoffs were spreading. To make sure he could get the team on board, Dean put the project on hold for a few weeks, stopping all technical discussions with suppliers. For three weeks, he focused solely on working with his communications team. Here's what they did together:

- They created documents to explain what a robot is and what it can and can't do. They also gathered video case studies (online) from various companies showing workers who explained their initial concerns and how they felt after the robots had been deployed.

- They prepared a list of FAQs, and did their best to include responses to workers' main concerns.

- They held a team meeting, where they explained to everyone who might be affected by the robots why the company was interested in robots (ergonomics, productivity, difficulty finding manual labour), how the robots would be deployed, and how different team members would be involved.

- Then they shared their collection of documents and video case studies with the team so members could consult it on their own.

- They left their office doors open, but they didn't just wait for people to drop by. They also organized one-on-one meetings with team members to address any lingering questions and concerns.

PHASE 1: DESIGN

You've done the prep work, and now it's time to enter the design phase.

When I say "prep work," what I mean is that the design phase's **input** consists of:

- The definition of the project's scope
- Your schedule
- Your list of team members and their roles

In this section, you'll be working through the following steps:

A. Manual task map and layout

B. Robotic task map and layout

C. Manual-robotic comparison

D. Finalize the robotic cell concept

When you've completed these steps, what you'll have is the design phase's *output*:

- The robotic cell plan
- The equipment for the robotic cell—delivered and ready to be assembled

Fig. 14 depicts a flowchart of the design phase.

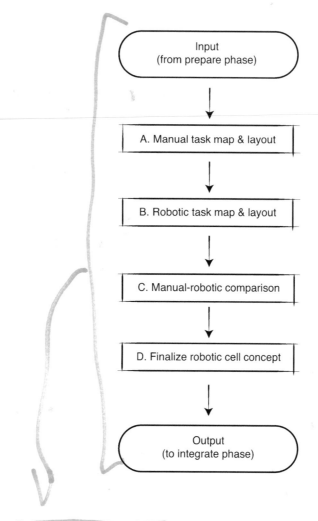

Fig. 14: Design phase overview.

Let's start with those two "mapping" steps, manual task mapping and robotic task mapping. These maps have the same underlying philosophy as lean manufacturing's concept of *value stream mapping* (see glossary).

In lean manufacturing, every improvement project starts with a map of the current value stream (see Fig. 15).

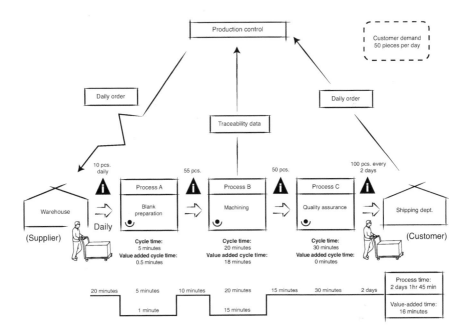

Fig. 15: Example of a simplified value stream map.

Using Fig. 15 as an example, here's how the map is created:

1. Identify who the **customer** is for a specific process and how the customer defines **value**.

   In this example, the "customer" is the shipping department. What the shipping department needs is 50 parts a day.

2. Break the process down into its various **steps**. Within each step, identify **value-added** and **non-value-added** tasks, and measure how long they take.

   There are three main steps in our example: blank preparation, machining and quality assurance. For each of them, it's possible to measure the time of value-added tasks and of non-value-added tasks. The time to transport the parts from one step to another is also noted. A line at the bottom of the map illustrates the total cycle time of each step and the value-added time portion of it.

3. Describe what (and how) **information** is transmitted among the different participants in the value creation chain.

In this particular machine shop, the production control will receive information electronically from the shipping department requesting the parts. This in turn will send information electronically to the warehouse team so they will prepare their delivery to the blank preparation operator. The machining center sends back some information to the production control electronically for traceability purposes.

Once you have the initial value stream map, you can create a new map of the ideal process. The "current" map and the "ideal" map are the basis of your project plan.

That's exactly what we're going to do for your robotic cell. In lean robotics, the "current" map is of the manual task map, and the "ideal" map is of the robotic task map.

The manual task map will be your starting point for understanding how the existing output is produced. Then your robotic task map will define how the robot can produce your desired output.

Once you have the two maps, you can proceed to the manual-robotic comparison step, where you'll find out what you need to do to transition to a robotic cell.

A. MANUAL TASK MAP AND LAYOUT

One trap we too often fall into is starting to look for a solution without having clearly defined the problem. We jump back and forth between trying to understand the current process and suggesting technical ways to accomplish it with a robot, which very soon becomes confusing. We should start by doing the manual task map, which is a static snapshot of the starting point from which we will work to improve.

Manual task mapping is a lot of work up front, but it will save you far more work down the road by letting you see the problem more clearly and have all the important information at hand. By documenting the manual task first, you're helping break a bigger problem down into a set of smaller problems.

MANUAL TASK MAPPING STEPS

Whenever I visit a company looking to install their first robot—and I've visited hundreds over the past decade—it goes something like this. We sit down, the manufacturing engineers explain why they're interested in robots, and then we tour the factory floor.

I'm often bombarded with questions like "Look at this station, how could I do this with a robot?," "It's a pain to do this task, how can I get a robot to do it?," "How easy is it to add a robot here?," and so on.

To answer these "how-to" questions, we first need to take a step back and answer some questions in order to fully understand the current process. These questions are the same ones you need to answer to complete the manual task map.

The manual task mapping process is like taking the value stream map and zooming in on a particular manual station. This mini value stream map describes the same things as the larger one it is part of: who the customer is, how the customer defines value, which steps are involved, whether or not those steps are value-added, and how the information is transferred. These things constitute the **value creation** information.

There is one difference from a typical lean manufacturing value map, though. Although we'll be focusing on value creation in the manual task map, we also need to capture information necessary to later develop a concept of how a robot could do these tasks. Even though this **robotic constraint information** isn't technically relevant to understanding the value creation, we need to take notes on some specific aspects that will impact the robotic cell design, because robots cannot do everything that a human can do.

Capturing the information in the manual task map will save time in the later phases. The way it's structured (as shown in Fig. 16) means you gather all the relevant information—no more, no less—on the first pass. It will help you capture pieces of information that might seem like trivial parts of the manual process at first, but that will later prove crucial when attempting to do the same task robotically.

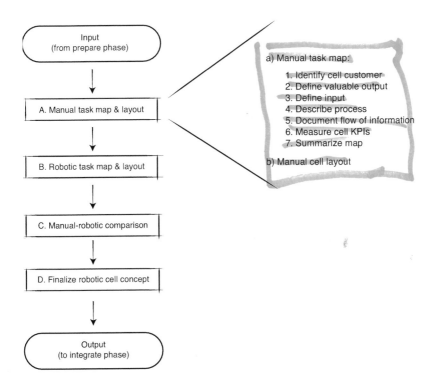

Fig. 16: Manual task map and layout steps shown in overall design phase sequence.

First, each step will be explained in more detail below. Then I'll walk you through an example.

1. IDENTIFY CELL CUSTOMER

The manual task map begins with the end of the process. This is aligned with the lean robotics principle of focusing on the robotic cell's output.

It might seem more intuitive to define the steps chronologically, starting with the first operation actually done at a station. But starting with the end means we focus on the real result we want to achieve: creating value for the next manufacturing step. It's important to keep this in mind to avoid getting lost in technical details of the process. In a factory, a manual station's customer is the next operation in the manufacturing flow. If your value stream map is the larger version that includes the manual process, the customer should be obvious: it's the operator or machine that receives the parts from the station.

2. DEFINE VALUABLE OUTPUT

Defining valuable output means answering this question: what input does the cell customer need?

Put yourself in shoes of the operator (or machine) who receives the parts, and complete the sentence "As the manual cell's customer, I need it to give me __ so I can __." For example:

- I need it to give me clean, visually inspected casing that arrives by conveyor belt every five minutes so I can assemble product SKU FTR002.

- I need it to give me part #AGS-002 with tolerances of .01 mm in that specific dimension every 30 seconds, placed on a fixture so the machine can do the surface treatment.

- I need it to give me a 10-layer stack of 20 x 20 cm trays filled with part #DJ2-3322 so I can package them for shipment to the external customer.

When you figure out the *what* ("I need...") and the *why* ("so I can...") of the next step in production, you'll uncover information that will have a significant impact on the robotic cell that will be doing this task.

Make sure you consider the cell customer's perspective when distinguishing the "need to have's" (what's absolutely necessary) from the "nice to have's" (what could make the job faster, easier, cheaper, more fun, etc.).

It can also be helpful to make drawings, pictures, and videos of the output process when trying to capture information at this step.

3. DEFINE INPUT

The next step is to define what materials and parts are coming to the station, and how the parts are presented. In this step, you'll aim to make a note of any information that could be relevant to your robotic cell concept.

Nature of the Part(s)

Here you'll capture the following information:

- Number of different parts
  - How many different parts are handled and/or processed at the station?
- Characteristics of the parts
  - Dimension
  - Weight
  - Material
  - Other, if relevant
- Variation in time
  - Are there changeovers at this station (in terms of the type of part being manufactured)? If so, how often?
  - Are you planning to manufacture new parts in the near future?

Drawings and pictures (including the correct scale) can work well, but may not be practical if you're dealing with a high number of different parts. In this case you can write a list of all the parts and their main characteristics (e.g., the main dimensions, the weights, etc.). We've seen this several times with tier suppliers who always make the same type of parts but in different shapes.

In other cases, the challenge will be not knowing the exact nature of the parts you'll be handling in the future, such as if you're a contract manufacturer. You'll want to work with a minimum and maximum range for various characteristics (min-max size, min-max weight, etc.). These projects often require tradeoffs. It's very expensive to build a robotic cell that can handle both the bulk of parts (that are all the same general type) and the occasional outlier (that's very different from the norm). So it might be better to reduce the scope of what's automated while keeping a manual station at the ready for outliers.

For robotic cells that will do assembly tasks, this step will involve a great deal of information, since it has to be done for each individual input (parts to assemble, fasteners, etc.).

Part(s) presentation

In many applications, the robot's main challenge isn't handling or transforming parts—it's simply being able to pick them up in the first place. As of the time of writing, robots still have a hard time dealing with unstructured things. If your parts arrive jumbled up in plastic bags tied with rope, it's no big deal for a human operator. But for the robots of today, picking the right part out of that bag is a nearly impossible task, especially if you want it done in a consistent and timely manner.

> When we talk about a robot picking parts out of a bag, we're only talking about part presentation—which is different from part *transportation*. Part transportation defines how parts are brought to the cell (e.g., a manual operator walks to the cell carrying the parts), but does not necessarily include how they are presented to the robot. So at this stage we're assuming the part transportation is taken care of, and we're only capturing part presentation information.

When documenting the part presentation information, make sure you look at the following:

- Are the parts singulated (individually separated with space all around them)?
- How do the parts arrive?
  - One by one
  - Stacked on top of each other
  - Arranged side-by-side
  - Placed randomly
- Are they packaged?
- Where are they?
  - On a table
  - In a fixture
  - In a tray
  - In a stack of trays
  - In a chute
  - In a bin (sorted or random?)
- Are they moving?
  - No, they're stationary when picked
  - Yes, e.g. on a moving conveyor

Until technology gets better, part presentation will often be an area where waste is added in the automation process to accommodate robots' limitations. A typical example is adding the non-value-added task of structuring the parts' presentation just so the robot can pick them. In this task, every time the robot is done working on a batch of parts, a human has to come and manually arrange the next batch to be worked on.

Again, pictures and videos work well to capture a lot of information related to part presentation.

A note on robotic constraint information

By the way, some of your tasks (both above and in the steps to follow) are only necessary because of robots' current limitations. For instance, the reason why it's so important to take detailed notes on the way parts are currently being presented is because right now, most robots are only able to pick parts when they're presented in certain structured, precise ways.

As robotic capabilities evolve, however, such detailed notes may no longer be necessary. To use the same example, this means that once robots can pick parts with near-human-level abilities, you'll no longer need to write down every single aspect of how parts are presented.

Anyway, this is just something to keep in mind for years down the road when robotic technology will be drastically different from where it is today. So until then, you should continue trying to capture all the relevant information during the manual task mapping phase.

4. DESCRIBE PROCESS

At this stage, you're capturing information on everything that happens between two points: when the input parts arrive, and when the output parts are received by the next station.

This can be the trickiest part of the manual task mapping stage. Think of a manual faucet polishing application, for example. The manual operator will pick the part, adjust his moves from what he originally sees, and apply various forces at various speeds until the finished product looks good to him. How do you document and measure that process to eventually program a robot to do it?

There are infinite combinations of processes and parts, and what's relevant for each of them will vary greatly. The good news is that even if you're not an expert in robotics (yet!), you are an expert on your process.

Here's what you can do to make it easier to create a manual process map:

- **Take videos.** Processes involve many dynamic interactions, so it's a good idea to film the process from various angles.
- **Have the operator talk out loud** and explain what he (or the machine doing the process) is doing. Ask him why he does specific actions. Keep asking "why?" several times to try to uncover the root reason. When you know the underlying reason why something is done, you can start being able to figure out whether a robot could achieve the same objective another way.
- **Pay attention to hidden tasks.** Some minor steps might be trivial for operators but surprisingly difficult for robots. These tasks may have become so ingrained in the operator's routine that they happen almost subconsciously. A "hidden" task like this might be doing a visual inspection on a specific feature of a part, making sure there's no more dust or oil at a given place on the part, or removing a burr on one part out of 100.

Once every step has been documented, identify which of them add value and which of them don't, and measure the amount of time it takes to do them.

5. DOCUMENT FLOW OF INFORMATION

The flow of information happens between the cell and other parts of the factory, as well as within the cell.

What information comes into the cell? Is it transmitted electronically, on paper, verbally, or otherwise? How does it affect the task? How does the operator or machine know what to do and when to do it?

Ask the same questions for information that goes out of the cell. What information is generated at the cell that simply needs to be passed somewhere else? How is this information used afterwards? Is there information that's not currently being transferred that could have a positive impact on other operations?

These questions also apply within the cell. What information needs to be passed between the operator and the machine?

Create a table (like Table 2 below) with the information, showing where it comes from, where it goes, what form it takes, and what it impacts.

Table 2: Template for documenting flow of information.

Information	Coming from	Going to	Format	How it's used

6. MEASURE CELL KPIs

Depending on what your goal is in using a robot for a specific station, you'll want to measure certain key performance indicators, or KPIs. Even if certain KPIs are not your main target for improvement by the robot, they might still be important, so you should note their starting values and monitor whether they stay within an acceptable range.

For example, maybe your main goal is to increase output capacity, but you also want to maintain the current cost of making parts at this station. So you will obviously want to measure both metrics.

Table 3 summarizes a few examples of goals you might have and the corresponding KPIs to measure.

Table 3: Examples of goals and relevant KPIs.

What you want to improve	KPI to measure
Productivity	• Cost to produce parts
Capacity	• Cycle time • Cell capacity
Quality	• First pass yield (% of output done correctly the first time) • Defect rate (as % of output passed on to the next station)[2]
Ergonomy	• Occurrence and severity of injuries or repetitive strain incidents
Inventory	• Inventory at cell ($ value of input parts, in-process parts, and output parts at the cell)
Human potential utilization	• Human wait time • Human non-value-added operations

7. SUMMARIZE MAP

The last step of manual task mapping is to summarize the key information in a clear and concise visual representation. This will give you an overview of the manual cell that is to be improved; think of it like an executive summary comprising the core information of a more detailed report.

---

(2) In some cases, the defect rate is automatically 100% minus the first pass yield. However, the reason why it's different here is because it's possible, for example, to have a 90% first pass yield and 0% defect rate if you catch and re-process all your defects before they pass on to the next station.

Fig. 17 shows how a manual task map summary might look (without the details filled in).

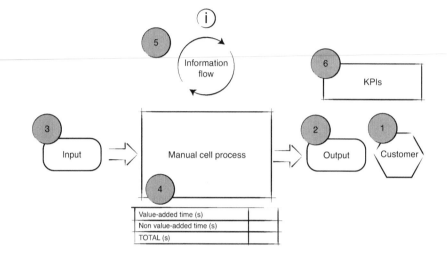

Fig. 17: Template for manual task map summary. The numbers in circles indicate the order in which the information is to be filled in.

In the summary map, you'll find references to all the information you gathered in the previous manual task mapping steps:

- Customer
- Valuable cell output
  › Customer's desired input
- Cell input
  › Parts
  › Presentation
- Process
  › Value-added steps and time
  › Non-value-added steps and time
  › Total process time

- Information
  - › Going into the cell (with source) and out of the cell (with destination)
  - › Exchanged within the cell
- KPIs

MANUAL CELL LAYOUT

Whereas the manual task map is about defining the current manual cell's sequence of operations, here we describe its spatial layout.

Often there's no work to be done here because businesses already have their cell layout documented. But if you don't, it doesn't have to be complicated: just make a bird's-eye-view sketch showing the main things in the cell, and take photos to complement your drawing. On the sketch, you should also include the dimensions of the main components.

LEAN ROBOTICS IN ACTION

> The following section illustrates an example of one company's experience with manual task mapping. We'll follow this same company in the rest of the cell deployment steps too.
>
> You can view this example in slideshow form, and download your own manual cell mapping templates, at leanrobotics.org.

The Acme Corporation is a (fictional) large contract machining manufacturer.

Last year they had a big order to fill and had to scramble to increase capacity. Their machine could only produce so much during the day, so their options were to have someone work overnight, buy another machine to run during the day, or integrate a robot that could work day and night.

The first option was no good. It's already hard to find good machinists, so they knew they'd struggle to hire one willing to work at night. Also, the machine they needed is expensive and has a long lead time. So they settled on the robot option, and had it up and running within a month.

How did they do it? Let's start by looking at their initial process for creating their manual task map.

1. IDENTIFY CELL CUSTOMER

The cell customer is the operator who brings the machined parts to an inspection station.

2. DEFINE VALUABLE OUTPUT

As the manual cell's customer, I need it to give me...

> → a tray of 60 parts every 2 hours (specifically part numbers AGS202, AGS204, AGS225, AGS400),

so I can...

> → take the finished parts to the inspection station (see Fig. 18).

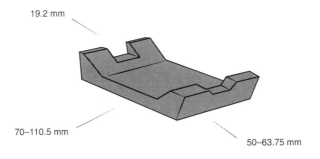

Fig. 18 : Example of a finished part.

Part(s) presentation

The following questions relate to how the parts are arranged at output (see Fig. 19).

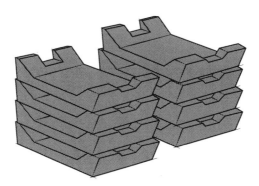

Fig. 19: Parts are presented to the customer (the operator) in stacks on a table.

Are the parts singulated? How much space is around them?
> → The parts are stacked on top of each other.

How are they packaged?
> → The stacks of parts are on a tray.

Are the output parts placed onto a moving surface (e.g. a conveyor belt)?

→ No, they are placed on a stable surface (a tray on a table).

3. DEFINE INPUT

Nature of the part(s)

How many types of parts are there?

→ There are four different types of blanks.

What are the parts' characteristics?

→ See Fig. 20.

Dimensions:

→ Max: 110.5 mm x 63.75 mm x 19.2 mm rectangular blocks

→ Min: 70 mm x 50 mm x 19.2 mm rectangular blocks

Weight:

→ Max. 0.36 kg

Material:

→ Solid aluminum

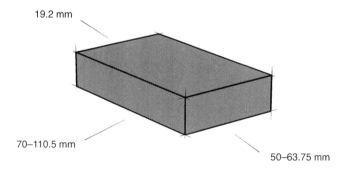

Fig. 20: Input part (blank).

Are there changeovers at this station?

> → Yes, two to three times per week.

Are you planning to introduce new parts in the near future?

> → Perhaps in 9–12 months. There will be a similar kind of blank at input, and it will be within the min-max range defined above.

Part(s) presentation

The following questions relate to how the parts are presented at input (see Fig. 21).

Are the parts singulated? How much space is around them?

> → They arrive stacked on top of each other.

What is the packaging?

> → The stacks are arranged on a table.

Are the input parts presented on a moving surface (e.g., a conveyor belt)?

> → No, they are presented on a stable surface (a table).

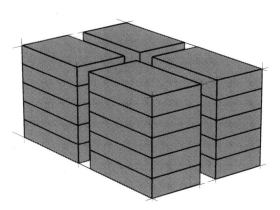

Fig. 21: Blank parts are presented to the operator in stacks on a table.

4. DESCRIBE PROCESS

The manufacturing engineer at Acme asked the operator to comment on the various steps in the process while he recorded a video with his phone. Since it's a continuous process, he had to decide what to define as the starting point in the cycle. He chose the state of the system when a finished part is present in the CNC machine's vise. So the first step is to open the machine's door to remove the finished part.

The process is illustrated in Fig. 22.

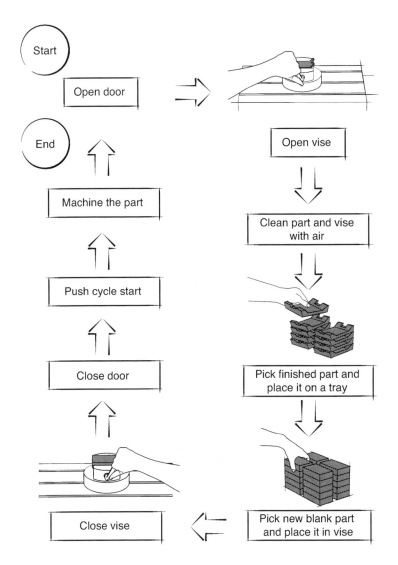

Fig. 22: Sequence of manual process.

Then each step was categorized as value-added or non-value-added, and the time to execute them was measured as shown in Table 4.

Table 4: Value-added and non-value-added steps in the current manual cell.

	Non value-added time (s)	Value-added time (s)	
Open door	2		
Open vise	3		
Clean part and vise with air	2		
Pick finished part and place it on tray	2		
Pick new blank part and place it in vise	2		
Close vise	3		
Close door	2		
Push cycle start button	2		
Machine the part		75	
Total (s)	**18**	**75**	**93**

5. DOCUMENT FLOW OF INFORMATION

In the current setup, all the information is transferred manually.

Table 5 summarizes the information needed at the cell.

Table 5: Documentation of manual cell information flow.

Information	Coming from	Going to	Format	How it's used
Cycle finished	CNC	Cell operator	Light signal	• Tells the operator he can open the door to remove part
Start cycle	Cell operator	CNC	Manual input	• Starts the CNC cycle
No infeed parts	Cell operator	Previous cell operator	Verbal	• Tells the previous cell's operator to output more parts
Outfeed full	Cell operator	Cell customer	Verbal	• Tells the cell's customer that parts are ready to be delivered to inspection station

6. MEASURE CELL KPIs

The most important performance indicators for the cell are:

- Real cell output—210 parts per day.
- First pass yield—97% (3% of the parts are rejected at the next station, which is quality inspection).

7. SUMMARIZE MAP

All the information gathered above can be summarized as shown in Fig. 23.

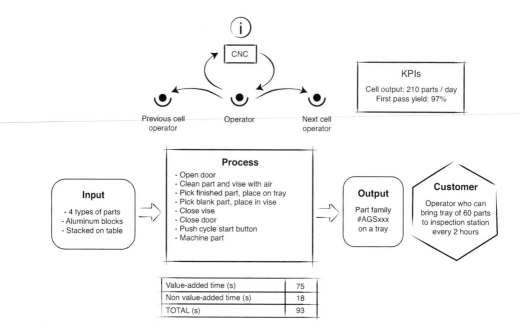

Fig. 23: Acme's manual task map summary.

CELL LAYOUT

After summarizing the manual task map, Acme also gathered information on the spatial arrangement of the cell.

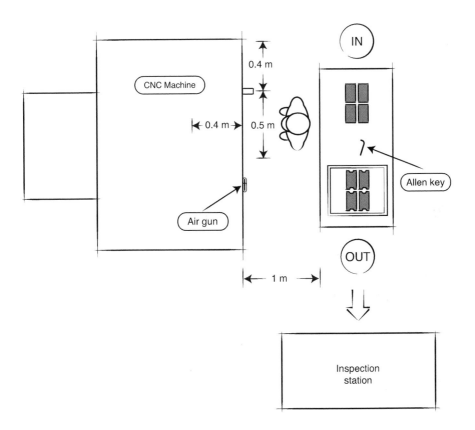

Fig. 24: Acme's drawing of the manual cell layout.

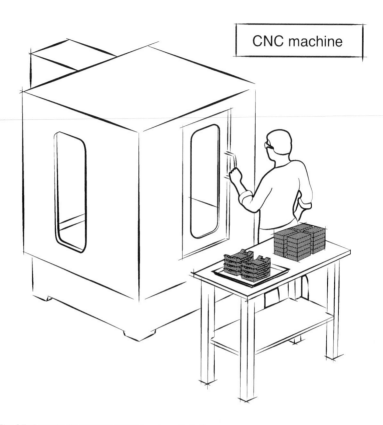

CNC machine

Fig. 25: Acme's illustration of their manual station.

Visit leanrobotics.org to view the example above, and a template you can fill in, in slideshow form.

SUMMARY

In the table below, you can find a list of all the steps to be done for the manual task map and layout.

Table 6: Template for defining manual task map and layout.

Steps	Information to capture
MANUAL CELL MAP	
1. Identify cell customer	Where do the parts go when the station is done with them?
2. Define valuable output	What are the qualities of a "good input" for the next station? In other words, how does the customer define value? • Parts and their specifications • Parts presentation method • Cadence/cycle time
3. Define input	What is coming in to this station? • Parts and their specifications • Parts presentation method • Cadence/cycle time
4. Describe process	How are the parts processed? • Which steps are done manually? • Which steps are value-added? Which are not?
5. Document flow of information	• What information is used at the station? • Where does it come from? In which form? • What information is produced and transferred from the station? Where, and in which form? • What information is exchanged within the cell?
6. Measure KPIs	• What are the KPIs and their target values? • How will the KPIs be measured? Example KPIs include: • Cost of producing parts • Cycle time • Inventory at cell
7. Summarize map	• Combine all the previous information in a visual representation of the map.

Steps	Information to capture
MANUAL CELL LAYOUT	
Sketch current layout	• What is the current spatial arrange-ment of the station?

B. ROBOTIC TASK MAP AND LAYOUT

The thing about robotic task mapping is you can't complete it without knowing the layout—but you also can't complete the layout without knowing the task map! So you'll be working on these two components together.

The robotic task map takes the same structure as the manual map, and is summarized in Fig. 26.

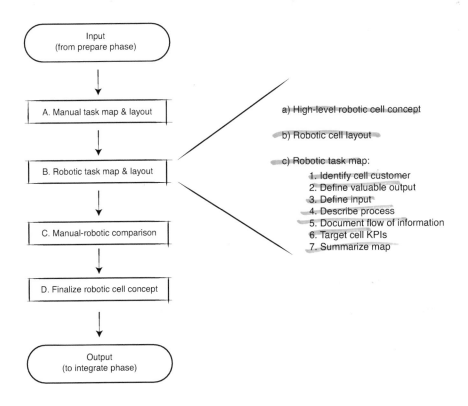

Fig. 26: Robotic cell concept, layout, and task map steps shown in overall design phase sequence.

Before doing the robotic task map, you first need a high-level robotic cell concept that describes the cell constituents and task sequence.

HIGH-LEVEL ROBOTIC CELL CONCEPT

At this stage, you don't want to do a detailed design of the robotic cell. The goal is just to have at least one cell concept that you'll be able to compare with the current manual process so you can figure out if it's worth pursuing the concept. Only then will you proceed to create a final robotic cell concept in all its glorious detail.

You start your high-level robotic cell concept work by identifying the main parts of the robotic cell that are not present in the manual cell. These components include:

- **The robot**—Which brand and model of robot has the right specifications for the process (reach, payload, speed, repeatability, compatibility with tool, etc.)?

- **Tooling**—What tooling, both on the robot and elsewhere in the cell, is necessary for the process?

- **Sensors**—Do you intend to do closed loop control or logic-based programming using sensor data? Sensors can be simple, like limit switches, or more complex, like vision systems and force-torque sensors.

- **Safety measures**—Will you choose power and force limiting, fencing, safety sensors, or something else?

- **Software**—Will you use external software to manage the process and/or program the robot?

You will have to evaluate the specifications of every component that will be added to the robot—the tooling, sensors, safeguards, and software.

You'll also have to consider how these things will interface with your chosen robot. Don't underestimate the effort (non-value-added effort!) needed to interface two machines that were not meant to work together.

The next step is describing the high-level sequence that the robot will do. The sequence description should include the following:

- **Part infeed technique**—How will the parts be presented to the robot? This decision relates to your choice of tooling and sensors. You'll need to find the right balance of cost, flexibility, and complexity for your situation.

- **Part outfeed technique**—How will the parts be presented to the cell customer? Can you even present the parts to the customer, or must you add an intermediary step between the robotic cell and the original customer (such as some secondary inspection task)?

- **Process sequence**—How will the robot execute the process? Write the process down in bullet point form.

- **Information flow**—What information will need to be exchanged within the cell, and between the cell and other parts of the factory?

If you lack either the time or expertise to complete this robotic concept work, you can go to system integrators or robotic vendors.

Having your prepared manual task map in hand will save a great deal of communication time. After just a few small clarifications, vendors and system integrators will be able to start developing concepts with you right away.

What you want to do with the concepts is entirely up to you. Again, your first robotic cell is unlikely to be your last. Using the right external help can be a great way to get a good short-term result while building valuable long-term expertise.

ROBOTIC CELL LAYOUT

The cell layout is a bird's eye view of the robotic cell showing how parts are placed with respect to each other and with their direct environment in space. Use a representation with similar references as your manual cell layout so they'll be easy to compare.

You probably drafted a sketch of the robotic cell layout while working on your robotic cell concept; but if you didn't, now's the time to create it.

ROBOTIC TASK MAPPING STEPS

The template for the robotic task map is the same as for the manual task map.

With the concept work done, by this point you'll have defined a good portion of the information that will be included in the robotic task map. The robotic task mapping steps are where you'll complete this information.

1. IDENTIFY CELL CUSTOMER

Sometimes certain aspects of the manual process are not good candidates for automation. You might realize you need to split up the process and robotize just a part of it, leaving the complex portion to an operator—in which case the robotic cell's customer might differ from the manual cell's.

For example:

- **Assembly**—You map a manual assembly task that provides a completely assembled product to its customer, a packaging station. The robotic cell you're planning to implement can only do the first five assembly tasks, leaving the last two high-dexterity tasks to a manual operator. Here the robotic cell's customer is the human operator, whereas the manual cell's customer was the packaging station.

- **Inspection**—The robot can do the value-added process (e.g., welding or polishing) but you still need a human operator to do a visual inspection of the parts. In this case, the robotic cell's customer is the operator who will do the visual inspection, whereas the manual cell's customer was the station receiving the cell's output parts.

- **Packaging**—A robot might not be able to package the parts to be sent to the next station if they need to be precisely or tightly slotted into their packages. In cases like this, the robotic cell's customer might be a human packager.

It is possible to have things the other way around, if your robot is capable of doing *more* than the current manual cell process. When that happens, you can extend beyond the initial customer to a new one further down the line.

2. DEFINE VALUABLE OUTPUT

Even if the manual and robotic cells have the same customer, that customer might have different definitions of valuable output. This is especially true if one goal of the robotic cell project is to improve the value of the output.

You can still use the same structure to define the valuable output: simply complete the sentence "As the robotic cell's customer, I need it to give me __ so I can __."

3. DEFINE INPUT

The reasoning that determined whether the robotic cell's customer is the same as the manual cell's also applies to the cell's input.

If the parts were already being presented in a highly structured and accessible manner, you can probably use the same input. The more unstructured the part presentation method, the more likely it is that you will need to add a part preparation step so the robot can pick the parts reliably.

A part preparation step could be singulating the parts and placing them in a fixed tray or chute, for instance. Another approach is to use a sensing system, typically vision, so the robot can adapt to the unstructured part presentation.

4. DESCRIBE PROCESS

Describe the sequence of actions that will be executed in the robotic cell. Estimate how much time each will take, and indicate which are value-added and which are not.

If it's your first project, it might be difficult to estimate the robot's cycle time or use advanced tools like simulation software.

If you're not experienced with estimating a robotic cell's abilities and cycle times, take good notes on all the assumptions you're making now. You can use this list of assumptions in the upcoming "de-risking the concept" step.

5. DOCUMENT FLOW OF INFORMATION

What information needs to come **into the robotic cell** so the robot can do the right task? Where will that information come from? What format will it be in?

- If the format is electronic, you'll need to define the communication protocol and data structure:
    - If the information is currently transmitted on paper or via a visual cue, will you need an operator to input it manually or trigger an action in the robotic cell?
    - What would it take to transmit it electronically or via sensors?

Ask the same questions for the information that goes **out of the robotic cell:**

- What information is generated at the cell that needs to be passed somewhere else?
- How is this information used afterwards?
- What data structure and communication protocols can be used to do this?
- Will new information be generated by the robotic cell that could have a positive impact on other operations?

Go over the same questions for the information exchanged **within the cell.**

Fill out Table 7 with where the information comes from, where it goes, what format it's in, and what impact it has.

Table 7: Template for documenting flow of information.

Information	Going from	Going to	Format (include communication protocol and data structure if electronically)	How it's used

6. TARGET CELL KPIs

In the manual task map, you identified the KPIs you will track in order to measure the success of the robotic cell deployment.

Now, decide:

- What are the targets for improvement—or the minimum threshold—for each of these KPIs?
- How will you measure and monitor them once the robotic cell is installed?
    - For example, will you manually track them, add counters to the robot program, or have remote monitoring of your robotic cell?

7. SUMMARIZE MAP

The final step is to summarize key information in a clear and concise visual representation, as shown in Fig. 27.

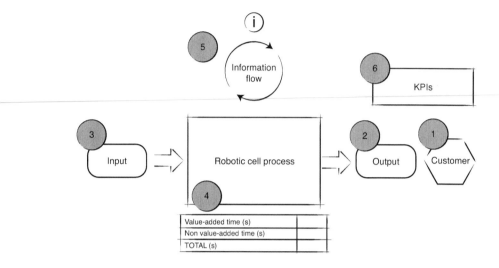

Fig. 27: Robotic task map template. The numbers in circles indicate the order in which the information is to be filled in.

LEAN ROBOTICS IN ACTION

Acme's high-level robotic cell concept is shown in Fig. 28. The cell concept includes the following components:

- **Robot**

  › Model ABC from the W-bot brand was chosen due to its payload, reach, ease of use, and safety features that negate the need for fencing.

- **Tooling**

  › Two grippers from supplier X will be installed on the robot wrist. This will enable optimization of cycle time. The grippers can accommodate the various sizes of input parts that vary from one batch to another.

› An air gun actuated by an electric I/O will be installed under the gripper that picks the finished parts. The air gun will clean the fixed vise in the CNC before blank parts are placed in the vise by the other gripper.

› In addition, the fixed vise will need to be converted to a pneumatic version that can be opened and closed via electric I/O.

- **Sensor**

  › Because of the various input part sizes, Acme decided not to use fixtures to place the part at the input. To help pick them precisely, a camera from supplier Y will be installed at the robot's wrist. Acme made sure the chosen camera has the standard driver and mechanical interface to work on a W-bot robot.

- **Safety measures**

  › Marks on the ground will indicate to the user that that he or she should not enter the robot's workspace. Workers will be trained on safety measures, and instructed to use protective equipment such as glasses and hard-cap shoes. The robot's movements will be limited to a certain speed.

- **Software**

  › Standard W-bot software will be used for programming. Drivers from gripper company X and camera company Y are provided for the W-bot controller.

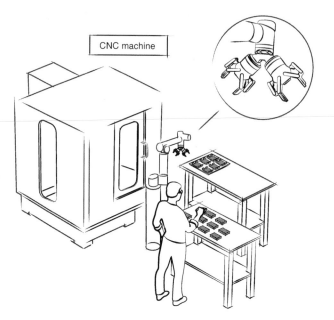

Fig. 28: Acme's illustrated robotic cell concept.

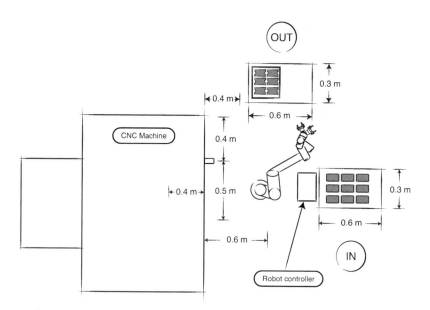

Fig. 29: Acme's robotic cell concept layout.

With this concept, the rest of the robotic task map can be completed.

1. IDENTIFY CELL CUSTOMER

The cell customer is the operator who brings the machined parts to an inspection station.

2. DEFINE VALUABLE OUTPUT

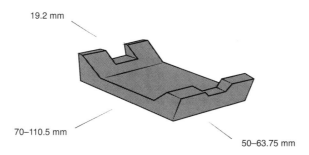

Fig. 30: Example of a finished part.

As the robotic cell's customer, I need it to give me...

→ a tray of 60 parts every 2 hours (specifically part numbers AGS202, AGS204, AGS225, AGS400),

so I can...

→ transport them to the inspection station.

Are the parts singulated? How much space is around them?

→ The parts will be laid side-by-side on a table according to a matrix (rows and columns) with enough space in between each one for the gripper's fingers to fit.

How are the parts packaged?

→ They are laid on a table.

Are the output parts placed onto a moving surface (e.g. a conveyor belt)?

→ No, they are placed on a stable surface (a table).

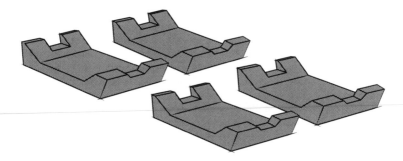

Fig. 31: Output part presentation in Acme's robotic cell concept.

3. DEFINE INPUT

How many types of parts are there?

→ There are four different types of blanks.

What are the parts' characteristics?

→ See Fig. 32.

Dimensions:

→ Max: 110.5 mm x 63.75 mm x 19.2 mm rectangular blocks

→ Min: 70 mm x 50 mm x 19.2 mm rectangular blocks

Weight:

→ Max: 0.36 kg

Material:

→ Solid aluminum

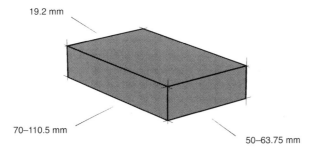

19.2 mm

70–110.5 mm

50–63.75 mm

Fig. 32: Input part (blank) in Acme's robotic cell concept.

Are there changeovers at this station?

→ Yes, two to three times per week.

Are you planning to introduce new parts in the near future?

→ Perhaps in 9–12 months. There will be a similar kind of blank at input, and it will be within the min-max range defined above.

The following questions relate to how the parts are presented at input (see Fig. 33).

Their chosen part presentation concept is to position the parts on a table and use a camera to locate them. This method seemed to be more flexible than the alternatives, since the vision system can locate different parts automatically, whereas a hardware-only solution would require manually changing the physical setup to handle different parts.

Although they had a hunch this concept would work, they felt they needed more technical work to determine whether this was the right solution (see the de-risking section in the upcoming pages).

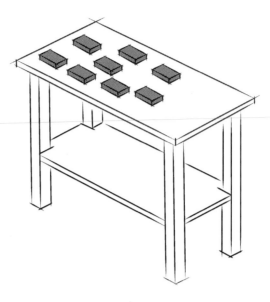

Fig. 33: Acme's robotic cell part presentation concept.

4. DESCRIBE PROCESS

Fig. 34 describes the overall process.

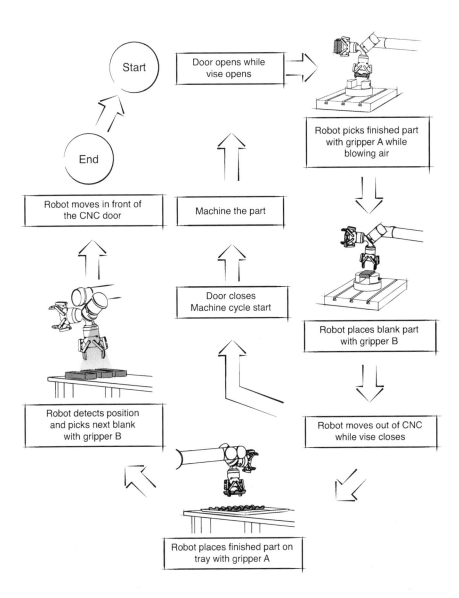

Fig. 34: Acme's robotic cell concept process.

The different steps are listed in Table 8. The steps identified with a *
are done at the same time as the part machining, so their time does
not add to the total process time, and hence their time is 0.

In the manual task, the machine cycle start step took 2 seconds because the operator had to push the button, but here it takes 0 seconds because it is done using an I/O signal (hence start time is immediate).

Table 8: Machine cycle time for robotic cell concept.

	Non-value-added (s)	Value added (s)	
Door opens while vise opens	2		
Robot picks finished part with gripper A while blowing air	5		
Robot places blank part with gripper B	2		
Robot moves out of CNC while vise closes	2		
Door closes	2		
Machining cycle starts	0		
Machine part		75	
Robot places finished part on tray *	0		
Detects next blank position *	0		
Picks new blank part *			
Robot moves in front of door *			
TOTAL	**13**	**75**	**88**

5. DOCUMENT FLOW OF INFORMATION

Table 9 summarizes the information needed at the cell.

Table 9: Documentation of information flow in robotic cell concept.

Information	Going from	Going to	Format	How it's used
Close CNC door	Robot controller	CNC controller	Digital I/O	When robot is out of the CNC, CNC can close its door
Start CNC cycle	Robot controller	CNC controller	Digital I/O	CNC can start machining cycle
Door is open	CNC controller	Robot controller	Digital I/O	Robot can enter the CNC
Vise is open	CNC controller	Robot controller	Digital I/O	Robot can pick the part from inside CNC
Vise is closed	CNC controller	Robot controller	Digital I/O	Robot can open gripper to release part
No more parts infeed	Robot controller	Operator	Message on teach pendant	To alert operator that robot cannot find more parts
Outfeed full	Robot controller	Cell customer	Message on teach pendant	To tell the cell's customer that parts are ready to be delivered to inspection station
Dimensions of blank	Operator	Robot controller	Manual input in program via teach pendant	At changeover, to adapt gripper opening and camera parameters

6. TARGET CELL KPIs

What is the target KPI?

→ The KPI is the number of parts machined per day. The target number is up to 300 parts per day. (This is achievable with a shorter cycle time, cell running constantly during the day, and one input tray machined while unattended overnight.)

Acme would also like to maintain a first pass yield (FPY) of 97%.

How will the KPI be measured?

→ Using a counter in the robot's program.

7. SUMMARIZE MAP

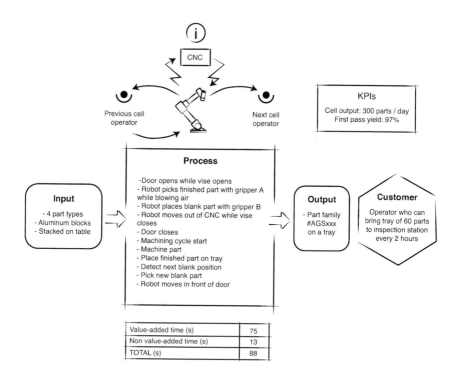

Fig. 35: Acme's robotic task map summary.

SUMMARY

Table 10 summarizes the steps that are executed to define the robotic task map after the high-level robotic cell concept has been defined.

Table 10: Template for defining the robotic task map and layout.

Steps	Information to capture
HIGH LEVEL ROBOTIC CELL CONCEPT	
Define concept	Cell components and concept.
ROBOTIC CELL LAYOUT	
Sketch robotic cell concept	What would be the spatial arrangement of the station?
ROBOTIC TASK MAP	
1. Identify customer	What's the next step after the robotic cell finishes its task?
2. Define output	How does the customer define value? • Parts specifications • Parts presentation • Cadence/cycle time
3. Define input	What's coming in at the robotic cell? • Parts (list of parts and specifications) • Parts presentation • Cadence/cycle time

Steps	Information to capture
4. Describe process	How are the parts processed? What is the sequence of events happening in the station? Which steps are value-added, and which are not?
5. Document flow of information	What information comes into the robotic cell, in which format, and from where? What information goes out of the robotic cell, in which format, and where to? Same thing for within the robotic cell.
6. Target cell KPIs	What are the target KPIs? How will we measure them?
7. Summarize task map	Combine all the previous information into a visual representation of the map.

C. MANUAL-ROBOTIC COMPARISON

You'll now be comparing the robotic task map and layout with the manual task map and layout. This step is like superposing two transparent slides to compare the differences. Laying the two maps and the two layouts side-by-side will help you find out:

- What the potential gains and losses are in terms of KPIs and waste.
- What the addition of a robotic cell will affect regarding the cell's customer, output, input, and information flow.
- What needs to be done to go from the manual cell to a robotic cell.

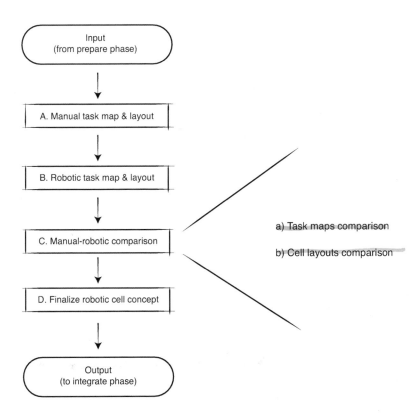

Fig. 36: Manual-robotic comparison steps shown in overall design phase sequence.

The first thing you'll do is a simple visual comparison. As shown in Fig. 37, you should place before-and-after images of the following on a board:

- Task map summaries
- Cell layout

This will make it easier to communicate your goals with the rest of the team.

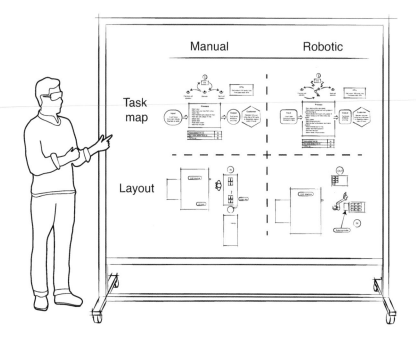

Fig. 37: Communicating with visual comparisons of the current manual cell map and layout and the future robotic cell ones.

You should validate the layout and robotic process sequence with people who know the current process well. These typically include the process engineers, station operators, and maintenance workers. Show them the layout and describe the process. Ask them questions like:

- Is anything missing from the sequence or the cell concept?
- Can you think of any exceptions, or envision any new scenarios the robotic cell won't be able to handle?
- Do you agree with our choice of the KPIs we want to maintain and improve? Are we missing any?
- What could go wrong?

TASK MAP COMPARISON STEPS

For every aspect of the task maps, you will compare the manual approach with its robotic counterpart. This will help you get a clear view of the advantages and disadvantages of the two approaches. You're sure to discover work you'll need to do in the detailed design and integration phases. By refining your view, you'll also be able to calculate a more realistic ROI for the rest of your robotic cell deployment plan.

1. IDENTIFY CUSTOMER

- Is the cell customer the same in your robotic cell concept as it was with the manual station?
- If it's a different one, will you require a new machine, new operator, or new tasks to be done by the current customer's operators?

2. DEFINE OUTPUT

Let's return to how the customer defines value:

- Does the addition of the robot increase or reduce the value provided to the cell's customer?
- Are we improving or worsening aspects the customer cares about, like quality, throughput, or consistency?
- Are there any downstream effects on the customer, or the customers' customers?

3. DEFINE INPUT

- Can you use the exact same part presentation as in the manual cell?
- If not, what needs to change?
- Do you need new part-feeding machines, passive mechanisms, or fixtures?
- Will these things impact the work of an operator? If so, how?

Think about the incoming part specifications and quality requirements as well. To have the robot work reliably, do you need to have more consistent parts? This can have some upstream effects that will incur some extra work but end up reducing the overall waste. Humans can deal with non-repeatable or dirty parts (although adjusting and cleaning them are non-value-added tasks). If your robot can't perform these tasks when needed, you'll be forced to address the root cause of these part issues, which could involve changing some upstream processes.

4. DESCRIBE PROCESS

- Does the addition of the robot improve the process?
- Does it reduce the amount, time, or cost of non-value-added operations?

Typically, robots will be better at repetitive tasks than humans, but worse at adapting to new tasks, so consider the following:

- Is the robot able to handle the parts and execute the process?
- Do you need external fixtures or accessories for the robot to perform its task?

5. DOCUMENT FLOW OF INFORMATION

Humans can deal with incomplete or unstructured data, like a manufacturing order in the form of a handwritten note. But when working with robots, it's better to send information digitally. Do you need to change the way information travels? You might have to do some more work upstream, but in the end, having a structured, digitized flow of data will reduce waste and avoid the risk of manufacturing defects.

Here are the questions to ask:

- In the envisioned process, will the robot have to exchange information with other machines inside the cell?

- Will some engineering work be required to make the machines "talk" to each other?
- Do the machines come with communication cards, or do you need to purchase and configure them separately?
- How will this information affect the process done by the robotic cell?

Your robotic cell might also generate new information that could be used elsewhere. Robotic cells are computers with actuators, sensors, and other data-gathering tools. Could this data be used to plan, track, or improve production?

If the robot is the only machine in a section of the production line, it can become a probe to measure how the line is doing, helping you implement continuous improvements. Depending on the point at which the robot (or just its program) stops working, you might be able to understand what the problem was: Was it missing input parts? Was the wrong part presented? Was the part out of tolerance (bigger than the design specification designated)? Detecting and logging these events can serve as the starting point for planning future improvements—some of which might not even involve the robotic cell—on the production line.

6. MEASURE KPIs

- How do you think going from a manual to a robotic cell will affect the KPIs?
- Will you need to change how you track them once you move to a robotic cell?

As mentioned above, you might even have the opportunity to do a better job tracking now that the robot is managing the process, if you set it up to automatically generate information in a digital format.

CELL LAYOUT COMPARISON STEPS

Just like you just did with the task maps, compare the robotic and manual cell layouts:

- What are the differences?
- Will you need to buy or fabricate new equipment, or move some equipment around?
- Will it impact other cells around the one you are working on?

As you can see, all the work you did to understand the manual and robotic cell processes made it straightforward to compare them. It is at the next phase—integrate—that the work will really start to pay off.

LEAN ROBOTICS IN ACTION

In this section, we return to Acme Corp. to see how they compared the manual process with the robotic cell concept. As you'll see in this example, during this exercise it becomes easy to spot the differences between the manual and the robotic cells.

1. IDENTIFY CUSTOMER

Same:

- The customer of the robotic cell is the same as the customer of the manual cell.

2. DEFINE OUTPUT

Same:

- The parts provided to the customer will be the same in the robotic cell as they were in the manual cell.
- All the same varieties of parts will be produced.

Different:

- The robot will not be able to stack the parts on top of each other.

- The tray will need to be slightly larger to have enough places for the 60 parts.

3. DEFINE INPUT

Same:

- The input parts will be the same in the robotic cell as they were in the manual cell.

- The robotic cell will be able to pick the complete range of input parts.

Different:

- The parts will need to be presented differently.

- The parts will need to be separated and spaced on a single plane, since the robot will not be able to deal with stacked parts.

- This will require the operator that provides the part to feed parts to the cell three times as often.

4. DESCRIBE PROCESS

Different:

- The steps done by the robot will be different than the ones done by the manual operator.

- A manual operator will no longer be needed at the cell.

- Total cycle time should be shorter and more repeatable with the robotic cell (88 sec., compared to the manual cell's 93 sec.).

5. DOCUMENT FLOW OF INFORMATION

Different:

- Digital communication will need to be set up between the robot's and CNC's controllers.

- The operator will need to input the dimensions of the blank into the robot controller whenever there is a changeover.

- The operator at the input station will have to check the cell's infeed more often, since unlike the human operator, the robot has no way to communicate the fact that the cell infeed is empty. The same is true at the output.

6. MEASURE KPIs

Same:

- The first pass yield target stays the same.

Different:

- Production capacity should go from 210 to 300 parts per day.
- It will be measured using a counter in the robot's program.

DIFFERENCE IN LAYOUT

- The CNC machine will stay in the same place.
- The table currently used by the operator will need to be moved so the robot has more space around it to reach the picking and placing areas.
- Marks on the ground will be added to identify the robot's workspace.

SUMMARY

Table 11: Template for manual-robotic comparison.

Steps	
MANUAL-ROBOTIC TASK MAPS COMPARISON	
1. Identify customer	Can we provide what our original customer needs, or must we add an intermediary step?
2. Define output	Are we raising or lowering the amount of value provided to the cell's customer?

Steps	
3. Define input	Do we need to change how the parts are presented?
4. Describe process	Are we improving the process? Are we reducing non-value-added operations?
5. Document flow of information	Do we need to change the information that is input or output? Are we generating new information that could be useful elsewhere? Do we change the information being communicated within the cell?
6. Measure KPIs	How does the robotic cell affect the KPIs themselves? Do the KPIs need to be tracked differently?
MANUAL-ROBOTIC LAYOUTS COMPARISON	
1.	Do we need to add, modify, or move equipment in this cell or neighboring cells?

D. FINALIZE THE ROBOTIC CELL DESIGN

You came up with a concept, and compared it to your current situation. Now you're going to make a decision about whether or not it's a good project to pursue, and if so, what exactly it should be, using the steps shown in Fig. 38 .

I'll show you how to draw the line between what's acceptable and what's not for your MVRC. We'll start with some financial calculations, and then you might need to test some proofs of concept to eliminate uncertainty and de-risk your final design. Once this is done, and you've purchased and received your parts, you can consider the design phase complete!

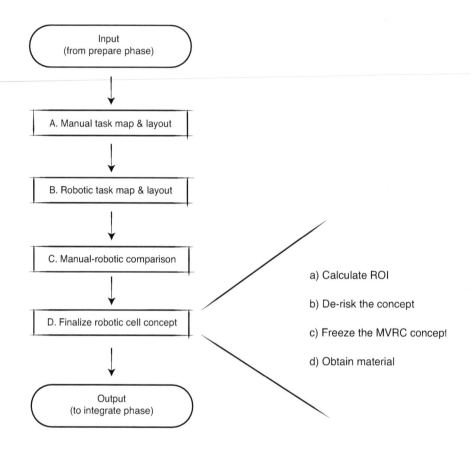

Fig. 38: Steps to finalize the robotic cell concept.

CALCULATE RETURN ON INVESTMENT

As with any capital investment in your factory, you probably have a process for calculating a return on investment (ROI) and getting the investment approved. The ROI is calculated as follows:

ROI = (gain from investment – cost of investment) / cost of investment

This is a standard formula that any company owner or head of finance will be familiar with. I will discuss a few things you should consider when you calculate the ROI for your first robotic cell.

At this point, you should be able to estimate the cost of investment as the sum of:

- Cost of material needed (as identified in the robotic cell concept step).
- Plus the cost of labor needed to do the tasks (for going from a manual to a robotic cell) that were identified in the manual-robotic comparison step.

If you're working with system integrators, the estimated cost of investment will be the quote they provide you with.

CAPITAL VS. INNOVATION INVESTMENT

Buying the components of a robotic cell is definitely a capital investment. You're buying machines that are expected to be productive over many years. But you should also consider your first robotic cell (or a new type) to be an investment in innovation: a project during which you will be building new knowledge that will benefit the company for many years.

Given that these two types of investment—capital and innovation—are present, let's break the ROI calculation down and look at the return for each of these two types. To do so, we'll compare two projects called Project #1 and Project #2.

CAPITAL INVESTMENT

Your capital investment includes all the costs of the project (labor and materials) up to the start of the operate phase.

Let's say you've done Project #1. It took three months to do the design and integrate phases (this is the time-to-operate). The materials and labor cost $125,000. Your goal is to recoup this amount is the shortest amount of time possible.

The sum of the production gains and cost savings (compared to the manual cell) is $13,889 per month.

Here is a summary of the project variables:

Project cost	$\longrightarrow$	*$125,000*
Monthly gains and cost savings vs. manual cell	$\longrightarrow$	*$13,889 / month*
Time-to-operate	$\longrightarrow$	*3 months*

From the time of the start of operation, it takes nine months for the robotic cell to reach the break-even point in terms of *capital* investment (which includes the design and integration costs).

project cost (in $) / payback (in months)

=

monthly gains and savings compared to manual cell (in $ per month)

Let's say you want to calculate the ROI of Project #1 after one year. What time frame should you use? In other words, what moment should be your $t = 0$? Should it be at the beginning of the operate phase? Or should it be at the very start of the project, the beginning of the design phase (as shown in Fig. 39)?

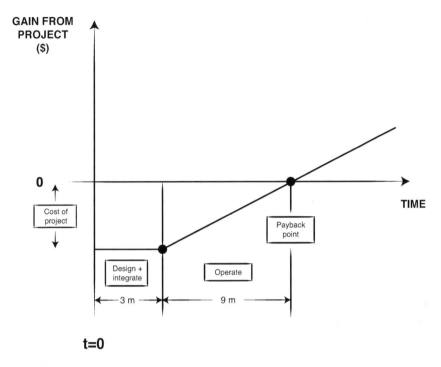

Fig. 39: Visual depiction of ROI calculation for Project #1.

START THE TIMER NOW!

One of my main motivations for writing this book was to reduce the amount of time that I often see wasted in the design and integrate phases of robotic cell deployment.

It's something people always seem to forget about robotic cells: your investment costs—especially in terms of time and effort—start rising from the moment you start the design phase; yet you can't even begin to earn back your investment until the cell starts operating and producing.

The cost of your investment ramps up once you start buying equipment to build the cell. The faster you can turn that equipment into a working cell, the sooner you'll see a payback.

Starting the timer (metaphorically speaking) at the beginning of the design phase is important for tracking the real ROI: the one that includes all the time and energy your team is spending, not just the price of the robotic cell's physical components.

Tracking the design and integration phase time (time-to-operate) is the first step to improving your automation team's productivity. It's how you'll estimate your team's capacity to deliver working robotic cells in the future, and it's how you'll practice continuous improvement of your integration process. When you and your team look at how the time-to-operate can be shortened, you'll discover areas where waste can be eliminated, making your lives easier and your business more successful in the long-run.

Let's get back to our Project #1 ROI calculation. If you calculate the ROI with $t = 0$ being the beginning of the operate phase, you'll get a ROI of 33% after one year.

ROI ($t = 0$ at start of operate phase) = (($13,889*12) – $125,000) / $125,000
                                                    = 33%

Now for the same project, if you set $t = 0$ as the beginning of the design phase, you'll get a ROI of 0% after one year.

ROI ($t = 0$ at start of design phase) = (($13,889*9) – $125,000) / $125,000
                                                    = 0%

This second method is how you should be calculating your *real* ROI, because you start incurring costs from the beginning of the deployment project, not just after it's completed.

So your real ROI after two years is 133%, i.e. (($13,889*21) – $125,000) / $125,000. Note that here the two year period is entered as 21 months because there are no production gains and cost savings during the three months of design and integration.

INNOVATION INVESTMENT

Now let's say that you've learned from this first project, and structured your work such that the next robotic cell deployment, Project #2, takes two months and costs $100,000 to deploy, and is capable of pro-ducing 5% more than the first one did from the start.

Project cost	→	$100,000
Monthly gains and cost savings vs. manual cell	→	$14,583 / month
Time-to-operate	→	2 months

This is a reasonable assumption to make because you're reusing part of the design and programming from the first project, which reduces the costs of engineering this time around.

The ROI calculation for this second project will be particularly inter-esting in three ways:

1. The robotic cell will start creating value for its customers a full month earlier.
2. The project costs 20% less (savings of $25,000).
3. The robotic cell produces 5% more than the first robotic cell from the beginning. Compared to the manual cell it replaced, this adds up to an extra $14,583 per month.

The payback point occurs 6.9 months after production starts ($100,000 / $14,583), making it 8.9 months after the beginning of the design phase. One year after the beginning of the project, your ROI will be 46%.

ROI (t = 0 at start of design phase)   = (($14,583*10) – $100,000) / $100,000
                                          = 46%

Two years after the beginning of the project, your ROI will be 221%, which (as you can probably tell) is significantly higher than the ROI of Project #1 for the same timeframe. Table 12 presents the numbers side-by-side.

Table 12: Two examples of ROI. Note that time in months is from start of design phase (not start of operation).

	Project #1	Project #2
Cost	$125,000	$100,000
Time to design and integrate (months)	3	2
Earnings (savings + additional production) per month (vs. manual cell, $)	$13,889	$14,583
Time to payback (months)	12	8.9
Earnings first 12 months (vs. manual cell, $)	$125,000	$145,833
ROI first 12 months (%)	0%	46%
Earnings first 24 months (vs. manual cell, $)	$291,667	$320,833
ROI first 24 months (%)	133%	221%

The numbers in the previous example show how the innovation investment in the first project can generate great returns on capital investment for future projects. The numbers in these examples are not exceptional. They're fairly typical from what we've seen of customers who have done simple robotic cell deployments.

Many of our customers have told us their second project took 50% less time than their first one. The waste reduction techniques described in upcoming sections can help even more to maximize the return on your innovation investment.

ACCEPT UNCERTAINTY, BUT STAY ACCOUNTABLE

Since your first robotic cell deployment project is partly about innovation, you won't know the precise values of all your variables from the beginning. This can be difficult to accept if you're used to approaching things from a "finance and engineering" standpoint, but at this stage, the "learning and exploring" side of yourself must prevail. All you need to do when you're getting started is evaluate whether there's a decent short-to-mid-term ROI, an acceptable amount of uncertainty, and reasons to believe that investing in robotics will reap long-term benefits.

But once the project is done—and assuming you might want to integrate another robot—then it's time to rigorously close the loop on your learning and evaluate the real payback. That is why you define the KPIs you'll track and their targets for the robotic cell. If you want to scale your robotic deployment efforts across the factory, you need to be able to track results and build a business case for new projects.

THE ROI WILL EVOLVE

Your robotic cell is like any other area of your manufacturing floor where lean principles are applied: it will improve over time. Initially, your ROI calculation for your first robotic cell will be conservative because you're focusing on the MVRC. But if you do continuous improvements on the cell to make it more productive, you'll likely see an increase in your ROI over time.

Moreover, your investment in your first cell will pay off while you deploy future cells, since you'll save costs and be able to leverage evolving technology. Again, your ROI for these cells will likely be higher over a longer time period.

DE-RISK THE CONCEPT

At this point, you might face some uncertainties regarding the feasibility or cost of the robotic cell concept. It might be worth investing some effort in resolving these uncertainties. Since it's better to find out as soon as possible if some aspect of the concept will never work, a small up-front investment here can save a lot of time and money with the remainder of the project. This step typically includes a "technical check" to make sure all the components are the right ones, and that it is possible to assemble and connect them together.

Write down all the questions you still have about your concept. Then answer each question with an educated guess that's phrased in the form of a hypothesis.

Go through your answers, and ask yourself:

1. How confident are you that this hypothesis is correct?
2. If your hypothesis was wrong, what would be the consequences? In other words, how important is it that this hypothesis be right?

Make sure you write your answers down (perhaps by filling out Table 13)—it helps to step back and observe your thoughts from a more detached perspective.

For questions where it's critical to get them right, but you're not 100% confident in your hypothesis, you'll either have to live dangerously (not recommended) or come up with a way to validate them.

Assuming you choose the latter, you should fill in the italicized sections for the relevant questions in the table: define a potential validation method and estimate its time and cost. Don't hesitate to turn to external vendors, many of which can perform technical validations for you.

Table 13: Template for de-risking a concept.

Unanswered question	Hypothesis	Confidence (low, medium, high)	Is it critical to have the right answer? (yes/no)	How could you validate it? (Define way to test and measure results)	Estimated time and $ needed to perform validation

Let's bring back our Acme example. Table 14 shows the questions they had at this stage of their project.

Table 14: Steps for de-risking Acme's concept.

Question	Hypothesis	How confident are you about the hypothesis?	How critical is the answer to concept?	How could you validate it?	Time and $ to validate it?
Will the camera be able to find the input parts reliably?	Yes	Low	Critical	Test with robot, camera, and parts.	Supplier can validate in one day of work; we (Acme) already have the equipment.

Question	Hypothesis	How confident are you about the hypothesis?	How critical is the answer to concept?	How could you validate it?	Time and $ to validate it?
Will communication be possible between the robot and CNC controllers?	Yes	Medium	Critical	Connect controllers, test with simple I/O exchange.	Robot vendor and CNC vendor can collaborate and validate in two days of work. Production line will need to be stopped to test CNC communication.
Will it be simple enough for the operator to enter the part dimensions when changeover occurs?	Yes	High	Critical	Robot vendor can conduct a demo.	Demo will take two hours.
Will the pneumatic vise work well?	Yes	Medium	Critical	Vise vendor can conduct a test.	Vendor can conduct a trial on CNC in four hours— requires stopping production line.

Question	Hypothesis	How confident are you about the hypothesis?	How critical is the answer to concept?	How could you validate it?	Time and $ to validate it?
Will we achieve the target cycle time?	Yes	High	Critical	Robot vendor can provide proof of concept.	Robot vendor can validate in two days of work. Will be able to reuse part of this programming for production cell.

FREEZE THE MVRC CONCEPT

In this step, you will decide which aspects of the concept will remain part of the MVRC. After this point, you'll aim to get through the integrate phase without making any further changes to the design. This will prevent you from falling into the trap of losing sight of the end goal and adding too much complexity along the way.

In the robotic task mapping step, you worked with at least one robotic cell concept. Ask yourself: for the things that could be changed about the cell, what effect would changing them have on added complexity, your KPIs, or the ROI? Did you discover anything in the de-risking phase that affected the cell concept? Now's the time to take a close look at these questions.

It's like conducting a sensitivity analysis with a financial spreadsheet: you change a few variables and see how the end result is affected. If there are a lot of ways for the concept to change, it might be worth taking a few variations as stand-alone concepts and comparing them.

Last time we talked about MVRCs, I mentioned how it's often not worth it to build a cell that can handle every type of part it could possibly encounter. Similarly, it might not be a good idea to attempt to build a cell that could execute every possible type of task you might need it to do.

Louis Bergeron, Deployment Coach at Robotiq, says you should keep the Pareto principle in mind:

> You don't necessarily need your robotic cell to replace 100% of what humans would do. It can be more efficient to have the robot handle 80% of the tasks, and a human worker responsible for the final 20%. In fact, a simpler cell that does 80% of tasks might cost just 40% of what a 100%-task-handling cell would cost, while being more robust!

The goal of this exercise is to identify your MVRC once and for all. How far can you go in simplifying the project while maximizing the ROI (or other KPIs you need to improve for the business)? Keep in mind that in robotic cell deployment, the complexity-cost relationship is not linear. Simple things can be very simple; complex things can be extraordinarily difficult, costly, and unpredictable to implement.

Think back to times when new technology was introduced in the plant. Were there any unpleasant surprises? Aim to be wise enough to acknowledge what you don't know.

Since the earlier your cell enters production, the earlier it starts creating value, it's better to keep it simple. Here's an example of why. Say you have a MVRC that will provide production gains and cost savings worth $10,000 per month (compared to a manual cell).

During the project, you decide to change the MVRC in a way that will increase the monthly gains and savings by 10% total, bringing it to $11,000 a month. Making the change means your cell starts producing one month later than the MVRC would have.

Earnings from the MVRC during a month	→	$10,000
Earnings from the more complex cell during a month	→	$11,000
Difference	→	$1,000

So you could have made $10,000 in that first month with the MVRC, but you chose to forgo that month and instead earn an additional $1,000 each subsequent month. That means it will take 10 months for the more complex cell to earn back the "cost" of the lost first month of production! This simple example illustrates the benefits of sticking with the MVRC and getting it in production mode as soon as possible.

While you're deciding what your MVRC will be, keep track of how you made your decisions, because these notes will be useful as the robotics team grows.

Also, you'll have to define exactly what a successful MVRC is. How will you draw the line between a work in progress and a completed MVRC?

The answer is simple. Go back to the robotic task map and ask:
- Is the robot creating what its customer needs?
- Are we meeting the KPI targets?

OBTAIN MATERIALS

At this stage, you will refine the robotic cell concept by making plans and drawing up a list of materials needed. The key deliverables here are the following:

- Final robotic task map
- Cell plans (to be used by people installing the cell)
  › Cell layout
  › Plans for mechanical components
  › Electrical diagrams
- Bill of material (to be used when purchasing)
  › List of suppliers and their part numbers
- High-level programming structure

By this point, you'll have completed the deliverables of the design phase. More specifically, you will have:

- A finished robotic cell plan.
- All the equipment you need, in your facility and ready to be assembled.

While you're waiting for equipment to be delivered, it's a good time to start planning the integrate phase.

PHASE 2: INTEGRATE

You start the integrate phase with the cell design in hand and the equipment ready to be assembled. At the end of the integrate phase, you'll have a working robotic cell on your production line, ready to start creating value for its customer.

The integrate phase's **input** consists of the:

- Final robotic task map
- Cell plans (to be used by people installing the cell)
- Parts and materials, all ready to be assembled

In this section, you'll be working through the following steps:

A. Off-the-line cell preparation

B. Production line preparation

C. Installation on the production line

D. Training

When you've completed the steps, here's what you'll have—the integration phase's *output*:

- A robotic cell that's ready to start operating
- A team of trained employees who are ready to manage the cell

Fig. 40 depicts a flowchart of the integrate phase.

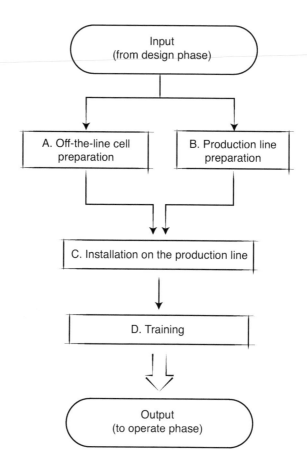

Fig. 40: Overview of integrate phase.

A. OFF-THE-LINE CELL PREPARATION

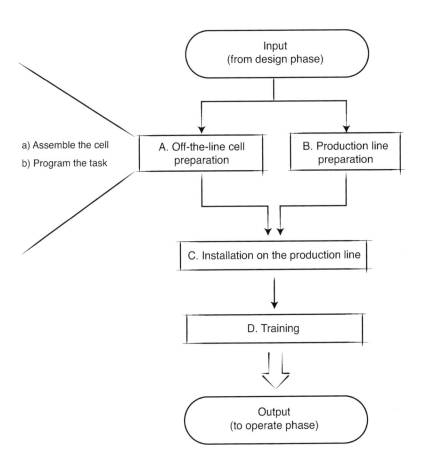

Fig. 41: Overview of off-the-line cell preparation step.

ASSEMBLE THE ROBOTIC CELL

To keep the production line running, you'll want to do as many of the assembling tasks as possible off-the-line. Find somewhere you can focus on the work, as the programming in particular will require concentrated attention.

Start by checking that all the equipment from the bill of material has indeed been delivered. Then gather all the tools you'll need and start assembling the cell following the cell plan. Along the way, you should be testing each of the cell components. It's easier to resolve problems when you catch them early and in isolation, rather than after they've been integrated with other components.

WRITE THE PROGRAM

You've already given some thought to the programming structure in the design phase, and if you developed programs in the de-risking step, you might be able to reuse parts of them.

However, programming requires an entire skillset in and of itself. Robots add an extra layer of complexity because you need to understand some physical robotics concepts on top of programming logic. Plus, as of the time of writing this book, robots have their own proprietary programming languages that must be learned in order to work with them.

The good news is that there are a lot of programmers out there and the principles of efficient programming have been well-defined by this community. There are tons of great resources on the topic, starting with the Wikipdia page (https://en.wikipedia.org/wiki/Best_coding_practices). However, the specific type of programming you'll need to work with depends on the brand and supplier of your chosen robot.

Although there's another whole section in this book devoted to waste reduction, I'm going to present a few programming best practices here so you can put them in place while you're still working through the programming stage. You should of course consider programming to be part of your continuous improvement goals, and you can go into more depth on these topics later when you get there, but for now this should be enough to get started.

PROGRAMMING BEST PRACTICES

Backups

You should have a robust system and process in place for backing up the application program and the robot's settings.

Revision control

Revision control means organizing the different versions of the same program. You must do versioning properly. It's key to figuring out where bugs were introduced in a previous version of your program, because you simply need to rewind your program history to find what change is at fault. It also helps everyone know which version they should be working on.

At this point you should define the program access as well: which users can run, read, or modify what's in the program.

Variable naming

Variable names should be as descriptive as possible so the program can be understood by everyone who will have access to it. Moreover, if people don't understand what a variable is, they may duplicate it without realizing. Adopting a standard for naming variables will help the different operators understand what they mean; remember to include it in their training.

Here's what Matt Bush, expert in robot programming at Hirebotics, says to do:

We use a standard naming convention of CustomerName_ ProjectName_Default for the default program that loads automatically. We then store our versioned programs in an archive folder. In that folder we use semantic versioning with major.minor.bugFix. We use the naming convention of CustomerName_ProjectName-vx.y.z.

We abbreviate the CustomerName and ProjectName so that they're not too long—generally 3-5 letters for the customer and project names.

In the "before start" section of the program we use a variable named VERSION to store the current version number so that it appears near the top of the variables list. This helps us to quickly identify whether customers are running the correct version of the program.

We do USB file backups at the end of each day of programming, and sometimes more frequently depending on what's going on.

Program testing

You should also define the program testing and release procedure. What needs to be tested to ensure that newly added functionalities haven't inadvertently broken any of the old ones? Test small parts and functions of the code alone. This way, you will be confident that these portions of code are working properly.

Structured Program

A logically structured program will improve readability, which pays off when training, debugging, and making future improvements.

Annick Mottard, Product Specialist at Robotiq, advises:

Having a general structure rather than a very specific one will make the program easier to adjust, modify, and improve. Also, the more specific the program is, the more difficult it is for someone else to work with you on the coding. If this is your first robotic cell deployment, chances are it will not be your last. A general code will help you code the upcoming ones and may be usable in a future robotic cell that has a similar application.

When you first start coding your robotic cell program, it's normal to have a very specific program. Don't worry, you're simply figuring out how to make all the elements talk to each other and how to implement your high-level logic sequence. Once you have that all figured out and clear in your head, put it down on paper. Write your clearer programming sequence on paper and then—I'm sorry to say—you might have to start your programming over again. This back and forth is normal and, trust me, it will save much more time and effort in the end compared to if you continued with your first, very specific, program version.

You can speed up future development with reusable building blocks. Break a program down into small, logical, stand-alone blocks. Use functions/macros to encapsulate abstract code under more comprehensible names. If you repeat a series of instructions in many places in your program, that's a good sign that these instructions should become a function. Use folders to organize your functions and programs so they're easier to find and manage.

Program comments

Clean, up-to-date, and well-commented code will speed up development. Programmers will spend less time trying to figure out the purpose of various sections. To keep the program easy to follow, use comments to describe what's happening in each section of the program's structure.

ROBOTICS-SPECIFIC PROGRAMMING ADVICE

Programming a robot is somewhat different from programming a computer or consumer mobile device.

Preserve the safety of people and equipment

Your program is what causes the robot and other parts of the cell to move. You can injure yourself or someone else—perhaps critically with high-payload robots and dangerous processes—if the wrong commands are introduced without being properly tested.

There's also a risk of inadvertently programming the robot to self-destruct. A typical example is introducing a waypoint on the other side of a table so the robot, unaware of itself, hits its tooling on the hard surface of the table and breaks it. In cases like these, it would have been a good idea to test the robot at low speed first.

Work around your lack of test environment

In software enterprises, there are usually three environments for creating and deploying new code:

1. Development environment
2. Test environment (which replicates the production environment)
3. Production environment

Programmers develop in the development environment, and test the program without impacting production in the test environment. Once everything in the test environment program is debugged, it is eventually pushed into production.

With your robotic cell, you likely won't have the luxury of development and test environments. In software programming, it costs next to nothing to set up an environment, but the same cannot be said with robotic cells due to the price of their hardware.

In the ideal scenario, you would have one robotic cell to be used for production, and then another robotic cell—identical to the first one—set up for development and testing. But unless you have several robots to be installed with the same setup in your factory, multiple environments are probably far too expensive.

Consequently, your versioning becomes even more important. It must be easy to roll back to a previous version if the new one creates a problem. Moreover, you should be able to restore a previous version quickly so as to reduce costs associated with production line downtime. Depending on what you make and whether you need to stop the line every time you do a program update, the costs of switching versions can be high.

Simulation and off-the-line programming can be useful tools for reducing these high costs. However, when we view robots through the lens of the *people before robots* principle, there are two potential problems with simulations. First is complexity: simulation and off-the-line programming tools still require a high level of technical know-how as of today.

Second is their lack of agility. If you're deploying a robot using the bottom-up, robot-as-a-tool approach, you probably don't have a digital representation of the robotic cell. So before you can do any simulation, you'll need to come up with that representation: a complete 3D model of the robotic cell, tooling, parts, sequence, etc. However, creating this representation entails additional non-value-added work, which will likely cancel out any efficiency gain that the simulation could provide.

Recognize that the program is inherently tied to the hardware

In robotics, programs are always made to work with specific versions and configurations of hardware. A new "hardware version" can be the result of a firmware update on a component or a modification to the actual mechanical or electrical setup.

In most cases, the robot's controller has to connect with other items like a machine, a conveyor, other sensors, etc. This makes the testing and the management of errors and exceptions quite tricky. For instance, if an error in the program or a power surge arises, the robot could stop at any point in its sequence. You need to implement ways to recover from these errors without damaging the hardware or the part the robot is working on.

Also, in interfacing with other machines, you should again try to encapsulate communication modules in functions with readable names. This will prevent you from having to decrypt abstract I/O addressing and values.

B. LINE PREPARATION

For the most part, preparing the production line to receive the robotic cell can be done in parallel with the previous step. What needs to be done at this phase should be clear from the manual-robotic comparison that was done in the design phase. You'll want to coordinate this phase with your line operators to minimize the number of times you have to halt the production line.

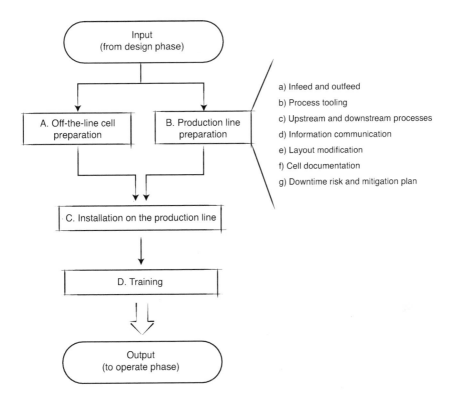

Fig. 42: Overview of production line preparation steps.

Infeed and outfeed

Will the robotic cell accept parts the same way they're presented in the manual cell, or do you need to build specific part-presentation devices? The same question goes for the outfeed. Can the robotic cell output the same thing as the current manual process, or are modifications required? If you have new infeed and outfeed processes, you'll want to test them in the off-the-line setup.

Process tooling

By "process tooling," I don't mean the tooling on the robot itself—that falls under the robotic cell installation category. I mean the fixed tooling that's already part of the manual cell's process. Will you need to replace manual tools used by an operator with an actuated tool? Think of clamps for welding or a chuck for machining, for instance. It's sometimes easier to change the tools and use robot I/Os to control the process tooling than it is to have the robot use manual tools.

Upstream and downstream processes

Did you realize you need to change the process upstream to ensure that more consistent parts get to the robot? Did you decide that the way parts are processed will need to be adapted once the robot is installed? Now is the time to do these modifications.

Information communication

You might have to digitize the way some information is transmitted to the cell before you install the robot. This might involve adding or unlocking communication interfaces in the machines that the robot will interface with. It can also mean preparing other machines or systems to receive new information generated by the robot controller.

Layout modification

Go back to your manual-robotic comparison and address all the things you identified as action items. Move the machines and other equipment so there's enough room for the robotic cell.

Cell documentation

Now is a good time to record the details of your robotic cell, because you've not yet done the final installation tasks, but you're close enough to have an accurate view of the final cell. Take some time now to create the basic documentation, because right before the cell starts production, you'll need to train the operators who will work in and around the cell.

You should create a training document that goes over the generalities of the cell and explains what will happen during the installation-on-the-line step. Your training document should also include the following:

- Descriptions of the robotic system components.
- Safety rules.
- Basics of robotic cell operation—how to start and stop the cell.
- How to handle exceptions (and prevent exceptions from happening).
- Maintenance procedures.
- Troubleshooting, with a section on problems and their solutions—to be updated whenever new ones arise.

Keep in mind that what's listed above only covers the cell itself, not general robotics concepts that your employees may also need to learn.

Downtime risk analysis and mitigation plan

What are the potential reasons for downtime, and what could be the consequences of it happening? How likely are these risks to occur, and how severe would they be? Plan accordingly. For the high-impact and/or high-probability causes, you will want to be proactive, such as by:

- Keeping spare equipment in stock (especially if your cell contains custom-made parts or parts with long lead times).
- Forming agreements with equipment suppliers who can provide you with critical parts at short notice.
- If possible, ensuring you have the ability to stop the robot in a configuration where a human could step in to replace it temporarily.
- Setting up alerts that will let you know of potential problems early on.
- Defining a preventive maintenance plan (that you will actually execute!).

Keep in mind that there are more risks than just those associated with the robotic cell itself. Consider what might happen if only one employee knows how to operate the cell. What if that employee leaves or is not at work when an unplanned power cut occurs? Would someone else be able to start the robot safely from any of the positions it may have stopped in?

To mitigate this risk, make sure to have the following:

- More than one employee skilled at operating and improving the cell.
- A program and a cell that are well-structured and easy to maintain.

Finally, you should aim to keep your documentation accurate and up-to-date with your latest modifications. That said, you can never completely avoid the risk that your documentation will lag behind reality. Instead of depending solely on documentation, remember to always keep the robot program and the cell itself simple, organized, and clean. It's important for the teach pendant and cell itself to be easily understandable, no matter how comprehensive the documentation is.

C. INSTALLATION ON THE LINE

It's finally time to take the robotic cell from the pit to the production line! Your effort and creativity will at last materialize in a robotic cell that will start producing value for your company.

This is also a time when good preparation pays off. You want to minimize line downtime and make sure the installation is as trouble-free as possible, since you're aiming to give your key stakeholders a positive first impression of robotic cells. You also want to minimize demands on the automation engineers and other workers, since they'll be kept busy during this phase.

Before you install the new equipment in a way that will make it difficult to do the same work manually if something goes wrong, you'll want to test the communication between the robot controller and the other machines. Once this is sorted out, you can put the complete cell into place.

Then you'll be doing test runs and executing the MVRC acceptance tests. As you go through the tests, you'll probably have to do some additional debugging, process fine-tuning, and cycle-time optimization.

D. TRAIN THE TEAM

Why training is worth the effort

Training the team who will manage the robotic cell is perfectly aligned with the first lean robotics principle, people before robots. It will not only make cell operation and maintenance safer, but will also inspire your team to see the robot as a tool to be mastered, rather than a job-threatening machine.

According to Daniel Pink, author of *Drive*, the foundations of on-the-job motivation are "autonomy, mastery, and purpose" (page 80).[3]

Training plays a role on all three fronts:

1. Proper training will allow the operators to **autonomously** run, maintain, and troubleshoot the cell. Having control of the robot will prevent the frustration that might arise if they were dependent on someone else to run the cell, since they can simply jump into action instead of waiting for another person to arrive.
2. Training will increase the operators' **mastery** of robotics

---

[3] Daniel Pink, *Drive: The Surprising Truth About What Motivates Us,* Riverhead Books-Penguin Group, 2009.

technology. Learning new skills is stimulating and improves confidence.

3. Training can clarify how the robotics effort fits into the bigger picture, and how the operators are contributing to this grander vision, which is something people need to know in order to feel a sense of usefulness and **purpose**.

Skilled, autonomous, and highly-motivated operators are a boon to any manufacturing company. Well-trained operators will be able to maintain the cell properly, avoiding downtime. And when unplanned downtime does inevitably arise, they'll react quickly and efficiently.

Training also frees the more advanced robot users in your company to do greater value-added tasks. Your "tech stars" will be able to focus on high-impact design and integration tasks during the next robotic cell deployment projects, while other team members handle the day-to-day operation of the previously deployed cells.

Thus, your investment in training will yield a great return by making everyone more productive: the robotic cell itself, the cell operators, and the engineering team that works on future deployments.

Just consider the following hypothetical scenario:

The price of an engineer's labor is $90,000 yearly. Assuming he or she works 5 days per week, 50 weeks per year, the cost is $360 per day.

The price of an operator's labor is $50,000 yearly. Assuming he or she works 5 days per week, 50 weeks per year, the cost is $200 per day.

Cost of preparing the training: → 5 days*engineer's salary = $1,800

Cost of training 5 operators: → (1 day*engineer's salary) + (1 day*5 operators' salaries) = $1,360

Total cost: → $3,160

The robotic cell produces $1,600 worth of parts per day over 8 hours (so $200 per hour), and operates for 22 working days per month.

Here is the potential impact of training:

- If training can improve cell output by 5% (or cell uptime by 5%), you'll generate an additional $5,280 over three months.
- If training can reduce a single downtime of 5 hours to 1 hour, you'll generate $800.

And we haven't even put a number on another benefit: the boost to your team's morale.

Who to train

You will of course be training the people who will operate and maintain the robotic cell, but who else? You might consider some basic training for employees who can affect the robotic cell's performance because they work at other stations. Explain the limitations and capabilities of the robot to workers at upstream and downstream stations.

The upstream workers will then know to pay attention to the parts that are produced for or fed to the robotic cell. Workers downstream who receive the parts will also be able to spot potential defects or any wasteful aspects of the parts that the robot is producing. A shared understanding amongst the workforce will also facilitate future continuous-improvement projects.

How to train

Recruiting, training and coaching the factory employees is crucial for any manufacturer. The robotics skills needed on the factory floor are hands-on skills, like sports skills, and thus they require learning-by-doing. You can have the best baseball player showing you how to throw the ball in a classroom, and it will be useful to some extent, but to become good at it, you have to spend time in the field. It's the same thing with robots. Lean robotics adheres to the lean manufacturing principle **gemba** (see glossary): you need to be where the value is created, on the factory floor, to make real improvements.

How to teach: preparation vs. improvisation

"Can't I just show my team how the cell works, let them run the cell, and then discuss other issues as they come up?"

Well, of course you'll want to involve practical demonstrations using the actual cell in your training. However, I recommend starting with well-structured training sessions before you move on to the practical demonstrations. This will make it easier for trainees to understand the purpose of the demonstrations, and they'll be able to go back and reference their training documents if they forget something.

A strong training foundation will also make future informal feedback sessions much more productive. It's important to give continuous feedback to the operators in the form of coaching in the coming weeks, but having that background provided by the initial training ensures they'll understand what you mean.

PHASE 3: OPERATE

When you're in the operate phase, your robotic cell will finally be producing valuable parts for your company, and all your hard work will start to pay off, at which point you should feel a well-deserved sense of accomplishment. You (will) have earned it!

Note that the operate phase is a continuous loop (see Fig. 43), rather than a one-time sequence of steps to follow; but it's presented as a sequence of steps in the "ABCD" format (like the previous phases) for the sake of consistency.

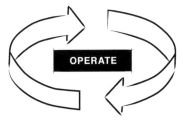

Fig. 43: The operate phase is a loop in which you continuously monitor and improve your cell.

A. STARTUP

This is when you'll be starting up the robot—a critical moment that is as rewarding as it is stressful. If it's your first robotic cell deployment, it represents a big change for the company, and something that will make a difference to many of the workers. Your goal here is to have a well-planned, well-communicated, and well-executed startup phase.

If the deployment is on an existing line, the installation and startup will momentarily disrupt production. Have a sufficient inventory of already-produced goods for the cell's customer while this part of the production line is stopped. Keep plenty of buffer time in your own schedule as well to respond to unexpected events. Especially if it's your first cell, be aware that some unexpected events are likely to occur.

You should also plan some one-on-one meetings with key stakeholders before startup. Be proactive to find out if they have any questions or concerns about the new working robotic cell. Don't let assumptions or frustrations build to a breaking point, when you can nip them in the bud at this stage.

B. MONITOR PERFORMANCE

What value is your cell producing? It's time to devise a way to answer this crucial question. Go back to the target KPIs that were identified in the design phase and implement the measurements methods you had defined. Once these are in place, look closely at the data and confirm their accuracy and reliability. You'll make a lot of decisions based on these data, so be sure to have a rock-solid foundation.

Once the data measurement methods are in place and have been proven accurate, close the loop with the KPI targets:

- Do they match what was promised by the MVRC concept?
- Are there any tweaks that should be made right now to reach the minimum level of target value creation or other KPIs?

These data will also be the starting point for any continuous improvements you'll do on the cell from now on.

C. AVOID DOWNTIME

At this stage you'll want to put in place the downtime risk mitigation plan that you defined earlier (inventory of spare robotic cell parts, alert systems, etc.).

Install a downtime logbook and give it a prominent place in the cell. Have it structured so operators can note the following information on downtime events:

- What was the problem and its effects?
- When did it start? When was it resolved?
- Who found out there was a problem? How?
- Why did it happen? What was the root cause?

- How was the issue resolved?

This log will be used for upcoming continuous improvement projects. It will also be useful for improving the training documentation and coaching methods. Finally, it can be a great source of feedback for team members who designed and integrated the cell, in terms of helping them know what they could do differently next time.

You might run into challenges for which you'll need external support. It's stressful when unexpected situations arise, but strive to keep a cool head. When we're stressed, it's even harder to make good decisions. Avoid the panicked "It's not working! Do something!" support calls with suppliers.

Instead, go through the following steps:
- Try rebooting the robot.
- Check cables, connections, configurations, communication parameters, the robot program, the power supply, and anything else you can think of.
- Try to identify which device or connection is faulty in the cell.
- Look for troubleshooting documentation concerning the device.
- If possible, ask another automation professional in your company for help.

If you do need to contact your supplier, first gather some basic information about the problem:
- What were the steps that led to it happening?
- What are the symptoms/effects you observe regarding the cell?
- Which tests have been performed so far? What were their results?

You should also keep the following on hand for your support calls:
- A photo or video of the issue—a picture is worth a thousand words, and visual supports will help your supplier fully comprehend the problem.

- All the paperwork you have concerning the faulty devices, assuming you were able to identify them.
- Information on the product's configuration.

This will prevent you from being mired in communication ping-pong (going back and forth without moving forward), making your interactions with suppliers more efficient.

Finally, remember to execute your maintenance plan. Most of us are guilty of waiting for problems to happen before we do anything, rather than preventing problems from arising in the first place. But out of all the types of waste, unplanned downtime is probably the most costly once the cell is in production, so do your best to avoid it.

D. CELEBRATE!

You and your team have put a lot of effort into the realization of this project, and most likely pushed the boundaries of your comfort zones. Once the robotic cell is up to speed, take the time to thank the people who have contributed to the deployment. If you have some before-and-after pictures or ones of the project in progress, put them on display. And if there are already some promising signs in your KPIs, be sure to mention them.

Have you noticed any workers whose perception of the robotic cell has changed? There may have been some uncertainty and fear before the installation, but after a well-done deployment opinions often take a 180-degree turn. Skeptical workers become the biggest advocates of robotics. They start looking at other processes where robots could be used. They might even give the robots nicknames! If you see that kind of change, invite these workers to share their experience with the team.

SUMMARY OF CELL DEPLOYMENT STEPS

The table below summarizes everything you've done so far.

Table 15: Overview of complete robotic cell deployment sequence.

Phase	Activities and tools	Valuable output
Prepare	Define project: • Identify manual cell to be automated • Set timeline Assemble team. Explain project.	Project summary, including: • Scope • Objective • Team • Timeline
Design	Map current manual task and sketch layout. Develop high-level robotic cell concept. Map future robotic task and sketch layout. Perform manual-robotic comparison. Finalize design: • Calculate ROI • De-risk concept • Freeze MVRC • Obtain materials	Plans and equipment for robotic cell.

Phase	Activities and tools	Valuable output
Integrate	Off-the-line cell preparation: • Assemble robotic cell • Write program Line preparation: • Prepare production line • Set up cell infeed and outfeed Installation on the line: • Install cell • Sync with production line • Define how to handle exceptions • Optimize cycle time Train team: • Document operation and maintenance procedures • Hold training sessions	Robotic cell and team ready to operate.
Operate	Launch robotic cell into production (startup). Monitor performance. Avoid downtime— diagnostics and troubleshooting. Execute maintenance plan. Implement continuous improvement projects.	Parts produced for cell's customer.

WHAT'S NEXT?

You've done what every innovative manufacturer does: perceived a business challenge, developed an idea, and put it into action. Congratulations on completing your first MVRC!

Now what? Maybe you're happy with your single robotic cell, and are planning to use your time to address bottleneck issues at another production station.

Or your next step might be doing a new iteration of the cell as part of your lean manufacturing continuous improvement effort. Since lean robotics is aligned with lean manufacturing, if you develop in-house skills, you'll be able to improve the robotic cell just as you would improve any other aspect of your line.

Another possible next step is to look at where you can deploy more robotic cells. Just make sure you've truly nailed the first one before you move on to the next. You don't want to be trying to sell the new project internally while the previous one is down for unknown reasons.

If you see the potential for several other robotic cells at the company, you need a strategy for scaling up your robotic cell deployment practices. To that end, the next section on scaling and waste reduction techniques will explain many methods you can use to scale robotics in your enterprise.

SCALING UP YOUR ROBOTIC CELL DEPLOYMENT

MINIMIZE WASTE

Robotic cells on the production floor must be aligned with the philosophy and goals of the whole manufacturing system: creating value for the customer with minimal waste. As we've seen in the section on robots' effects on your lean manufacturing efforts, the introduction of a robotic cell can both add and remove sources of waste.

Let's return to Acme's experience with deploying a robotic cell for the first time and see how much waste is generated throughout their project.

In this example, Jake is the manufacturing engineer overseeing the project. He works closely with his boss Dave, the factory's manufacturing manager. Dave has initiated Acme's robotic cell project because he believes robots have the potential to resolve some capacity and skills-shortage issues. He asks Jake to see where robots could deliver the biggest benefits to their factory.

Jake is an experienced manufacturing engineer: this may be his first time working with robots, but he's no stranger to introducing new technology on the factory floor. In fact, innovating is one of his favorite parts of the job.

Here's what Jake needs to do to get the robotic cell to work (italics signify delays and unnecessary waste):

- **Design Phase**

  › *Jake walks around the factory to examine various stations on the factory floor, and researches robot capabilities online.* He decides which manual cell should be automated with a robot: the machine load/unload application. Adding a robot to this station will reduce costs and avoid the need for a human operator to do some non-value added activities.

  › Jake maps the existing manual process at this station.

  › He defines the robotic cell concept (layout, parts, and parts presentation method). *This involves various communication delays, as Jake attempts to understand if the different components will do their work and if they can be easily interfaced together.*

  › *Jake is interrupted in his work and called to repair another machine that just broke down. He goes to identify the issue. It takes him a few minutes to regain focus when he gets back.*

  › Some technical aspects need to be derisked, so he contacts the robot and parts' suppliers to obtain the technical proofs of concept. *The vendors are able to do the tests the following week. Jake ships some parts for testing.*

  › He finalizes the design and cost projections.

  › He gets the concept and budget approved by Dave. *While he's waiting for approval, he works on other projects.*

  › He buys the standard components, and places orders for the custom parts to be fabricated.

  › Parts are fabricated and *shipped from the different suppliers to the factory.*

- **Integrate Phase**

  › Once all the components have arrived, Jake starts putting the robot together.

  › He tests whether the components are working properly. *Some aren't, so he opens technical support tickets with their suppliers.*

  › *He orders extra parts to resolve the problem, waits for them to arrive,* and then finishes putting the robot together.

> › Jake programs the robot. *He runs into a few challenges and can't find the answers himself; again, he calls some suppliers for technical support.*
>
> › After programming, he's ready to install the robotic cell on the production line. He schedules a *three-day line shut-down* so he can do the installation.
>
> › Jake notices something he didn't realize was happening before: some parts are arriving outside the picking zone of the robot. *He gets to work on solving this problem.*
>
> › He finally gets the robot to do its job reliably.
>
> › He teaches the worker who will operate the robot about its safety aspects, how to start the robot, troubleshoot it, etc.
>
> › At last, the robotic cell begins production!

Notice that in the design and integrate phases, the cell project consumed many resources without creating any value for the cell customer or company. So the delays and unnecessary waste in the above activities (identified in italics) should be eliminated insofar as possible.

In the operate phase, the robotic cell will start creating value for its customer. But even in this phase, there can be unnecessary waste.

- **Operate Phase**
  > › The robotic cell is now producing parts for its customer, properly and on time.
  >
  > › Periodically, *Jake checks the value displayed by the robot's production counter, and enters this value in a spreadsheet to track it.*
  >
  > › *Sometimes the robot stands idle because it's waiting for a part.*
  >
  > › *Sometimes the robot stops working because it has encountered an unknown situation (like parts that are placed too close together to be picked). Whenever this happens it takes a few minutes for the staff to notice, remove the unwanted item, and restart the robot.*

Were you surprised by how many tasks above are considered non-value-added?

In the first section below, we'll identify ways to reduce waste in the operate phase. This will ensure your robotic cell eliminates more waste than it creates, relative to its manual cell equivalent. We'll see that many lean manufacturing waste reduction tools can also be applied to robotic cells.

The second part of this section will describe ways to reduce waste in the design and integrate phases. One key message of this book is that manufacturers need to be just as obsessed about eliminating waste in the design and integrate phases as they are with eliminating it on the production floor. There is a huge leverage effect in reducing waste during the design and integrate phases, especially if your enterprise has the potential to use multiple robotic cells.

REDUCE WASTE IN THE OPERATE PHASE

Follow the lean 5S

The 5S approach in lean manufacturing is a useful set of principles for keeping a working cell organized and easy to visually assess.

- **Sort**
  Identify what is and is not needed at the cell. Keep only what's needed.

- **Set in order**
  Arrange what's needed so it's readily available to everyone who might need it. Make sure what's used gets put back in the proper location once a task is completed.

- **Shine**
  Clear the workplace and clean the equipment on a regular basis to keep performance levels high and check for potential damage. This is especially important for tooling, cables and hoses on robots, which can all be a source of downtime.

- **Standardize**
  Define what the normal state of the cell is. Ensure everyone can assess the state of the cell near-instantaneously, such as via visual cues.
- **Sustain**
  Maintain a normal state of the cell via continuous monitoring, feedback, and training.

Because robots have a hard time dealing with unstructured or inconsistent environments, you'll actually be forced to apply most of the 5S system by default, even to other surrounding cells. For instance, you'll have to keep the robotic cell's infeed clean and performing consistently, or else the robot might not even be able to reach the parts it needs to perform its task.

Reduce waste with task mapping

Looking at the manual-to-robotic cell transition through the lens of waste reduction will help ensure that you take that aspect into account at the design phase. Decisions made at that stage will impact the robotic cell's waste production for months and years to come.

You may have made some decisions that were good for the cell's KPIs and overall business objectives, but that also created some waste. One example is when you install a robotic cell with a high throughput to increase capacity that ends up generating some additional non-value-added tasks or waste at upstream or downstream stations (such as extra inventory, or manual tasks that take longer for operators to do). Make sure to pass this information on to the operation and maintenance team if it's composed of people who were not part of the design team. Otherwise they might perceive the robot as something that's only made their work more difficult, instead of something that's making the whole company more successful.

Reduce waste with downtime risk analysis and a mitigation plan

One of the biggest sources of waste with a robotic cell is when the cell stops producing. In the downtime risk analysis and mitigation plan step of the integrate phase, you identified potential causes of downtime and ways to mitigate them. Now make sure these plans are put in place!

You certainly want to avoid costly downtimes. But if they happen, you also want to get the cell back into production as soon as possible. To that end, make sure your cell operators are well trained on how to take control of the situation. The following information should be clear to everyone involved with the cell:

- Who has access to modify the robot's program.
- Where to find spare parts, and how to get more of them.
- How to access the system backup and reinstall it.
- Where to find information before making a supplier support call, such as:
    - System information (robotic cell parts, serial numbers).
    - How to get a copy of the program and error log.

Monitor the robotic cell

It's easy to tell when a robotic cell is down rather than working... but only when you're watching it. That's why you should have visual indicators or remote monitoring systems so you'll be alerted as soon as a downtime occurs. The time between when the downtime starts and when you start figuring out a solution is pure waste.

What about when the cell is working, but not as well as it could be? Reasons for that could include:

- Parts not being supplied to the cell on time.
- Outfeed not being ready when the robot has done its process.
- Unnecessary movements or processing by the robot.

- Errors that cause the cell to stop once in awhile, requiring the operator to go fix it (e.g., a part is dropped by the robot in one out of every 1,000 cycles).

Monitoring your cell's output over time can guide you towards finding the root cause of waste. And this can be the starting point of high-payoff continuous improvements. This is even more true if the robotic cell is surrounded by other operations that are not monitored directly. Then the robotic cell can become a probe that is used to assess the overall performance of the line. It can lead to continuous improvement of not only the cell, but all the other surrounding processes about which you'll indirectly gather information.

Error-proofing

In lean manufacturing, error-proofing techniques (also known as **poka-yoke**, see glossary) are put in place to prevent, correct, or draw attention to errors happening on the production line.

You have already introduced some error-proofing techniques in the design and integrate phases, such as when you worked on programming the robot using the appropriate sensors, logic, and tooling. Here we'll look at ways to error-proof in the operation phase via three specific strategies: monitoring, alerts, and prevention.

When your cell has only performed a few cycles, you have such a small sample that it's hard to identify all the potential errors against which you need to proof. These errors will become more apparent with a larger sample (more cycles). Monitoring the cell in the operation phase, and figuring out the reasons for downtimes will also help with error-proofing the cell (although of course, you're already doing these things as part of your KPI measurements).

The point where the robot unexpectedly stops will give you a good indication of what the problem was. Having a logically structured, well-documented program will also pay off at that point. If you've done these steps correctly, any operator will be able to look at the robot and understand what it was doing when the stop happened.

Another important aspect of error-proofing is making sure alerts will be raised as soon as possible after an error has occurred. You might want to link one of the robot's output signals to a visual indicator so nearby operators can quickly see if the cell has a problem. For critical operations, you'll want to set up a remote monitoring system that will instantly tell you when a stop has occurred, and provide you with information you need to take action as quickly as possible.

Drawing attention to errors is all well and good, but ideally they should be prevented from happening at all. That will help keep the cell running. Moreover, errors can lead to damaged workpieces and equipment, resulting in operational headaches and financial losses. To prevent errors, you'll need to combine information from the robot and the sensors with some programming logic.

You don't need to start with fancy sensors. The robot itself has readily available information you can use (tooling position and orientation, joint position, error messages). Some of the tooling output can also be used for basic checks. Combining this information will cover a decent portion of the problems that may arise in most applications.

Louis Bergeron, Deployment Coach at Robotiq, adds:

In my experience, the human factor is the most difficult to take into account in the error-proofing. Here are two example scenarios.

First, the operator pushes an emergency stop (or there's a power cut for any other reason). It could happen anywhere in the program. The operator can decide to continue the program from where it left off or to restart it from line one. Can the robot go back to the first point without damaging the tooling? Are the parts in the right place?

Second, the operator is making a production changeover (converting the cell from producing one product to another). Is there a way to prevent mistakes such as selecting the wrong program? What about mistakes with the input parts?

Keep in mind that when it comes to robots, it's easier to implement measures of drawing attention to errors than means of preventing them.

Most complex of all to implement are measures to correct errors on the fly, since doing so entails using systems that can self-adjust based on their sensors' feedback. (For example, you might use a vision system so the robot can detect if it has picked the right shape of peg, rather than repeatedly attempt to jam a square peg in a round hole.)

As with the risk-mitigation plan, the best error-proofing strategy is one that aligns the cost and complexity of implementation with the likelihood and severity of potential errors.

Cultivate autonomy

The fourth principle of lean robotics is to leverage your skills. This principle directly supports the goal of minimizing waste in the robotic cell. If your team is not autonomous, you increase the risk of having a non-producing cell for longer periods of time.

For example, when unexpected downtime occurs, a well-prepared, well-trained in-house team will be hard to beat in terms of getting the cell back to work the quickest. If you're entirely reliant on external resources, communication inefficiencies and transportation delays might mean it takes even longer to return your cell to productivity. Even if you do need to access some external resources to get it running again, having a skilled internal team will make that process much more efficient, because they can provide the right information to the external support team early on.

I've seen many manufacturers who had their cell installed by an external provider. At first, it seemed like they got a cell that worked well with minimum risk. It was only later, when their needs had evolved, that they realized there was a downside: not being able to change the cell by themselves.

A fairly common problem is needing the external provider to send a programmer every time the robot's program has to be changed. For example, a contract manufacturer of machined parts was forced to wait three weeks every time they had a new part for which their machine-tending robotic cell had to be programmed. During those three-week waiting periods, the robotic cell produced zero value. If you wouldn't pay an employee to sit and wait for three weeks, you should avoid paying for a robotic cell that will end up doing just that.

Summary

Table 16: Potential sources of waste in the operate phase.

Operate phase	
Type of waste	**Examples**
Transportation	› Robotic cell demands increase in transportation to or from it › As a result of the robotic cell addition, more items or workers must be brought to and from the station
Waiting	› Human or expensive machine left waiting instead of cheaper robot
Overproduction	› Robot produces too much for the next station to handle
Defects	› Unreliable robotic cell › Unacceptably low quality of output
Inventory	› Batches of parts build up at robotic cell infeed or outfeed
Motion	› Extra motions required to enable the robot to do its work
Extra processing	› The robotic cell does a task that should have been eliminated before converting the manual cell to a robotic one
Underutilizing human potential	› Highly skilled people required to do repetitive debugging or part-presentation work (e.g. picking parts off a tray and feeding them to the robot)

Operate phase	
Mura	› Changeovers outside of the initial scope of the project are difficult to deal with, adding more work for the team
Muri	› Processes outside the robotic cell components' specifications cause premature wear

REDUCE WASTE IN THE DESIGN AND INTEGRATE PHASES

Once you're done your first installation, you might be surprised to look back and see how as much as half the work you did in the design and integrate phases was ultimately non-value-added.

Maybe you spent three hours on a technical call where no decisions were made, or maybe you started assembling parts only to find that one of them was faulty and they all needed to be taken apart.

How can you prevent such waste next time?

If you plan to add more robotic cells, reducing waste in the design and integrate stages will have a huge impact on your overall ROI. Remember how we split the ROI calculation into two aspects of investment, capital and innovation? The waste reduction techniques below will give you a better return on your *innovation* investment, which in time will produce a higher return on your *capital* investment as well.

In this section, we'll look at waste reduction techniques that apply to both the design and integrate phases. First I'll describe the most important sources of waste in these phases—the ones I've seen come up again and again while working with thousands of manufacturers. I'll show you how to reduce waste here, and then explain how standardizing various aspects of your robotic cell deployment is the key to minimizing waste while you scale up the use of robots in your organization.

BAD SYSTEM DESIGN PRACTICES

A robot is not a self-contained machine. It interfaces with the world surrounding it, making the robotic cell a more complicated system than a stand-alone machine. With that in mind, here are a few missteps you should strive to avoid in your system design.

Not keeping the end goal in mind

The goal of the robotic cell is to create value for the next operation. This value is what defines the cell's target KPIs and specifications, so always remember where the specifications come from.

In the military, there's a concept of "commander's intent." Even though plans often need to adapt (since "no plan survives the first contact with the enemy"), the initial intent to "secure hill ABC" still holds and guides the actions of the troops. The same concept applies to your project: the specifications represent the initial plan, and the commander's intent is to create value for the next operation (the customer).

We too often see teams driving themselves crazy trying to achieve every last specification, forgetting why or how that specification was defined. If you're 5% away from the target cycle time, that last 5% might be very difficult to reach for technical reasons. But why was that cycle time specification defined? Is the end goal to increase capacity? Or is quality more important? Go back to the real objective and see if you're meeting the end goal.

Not having a clear schematic view of your complete process

Keep the whole process in mind. It's too easy to dive deep into a technical problem and lose sight of the complete system. The most important thing is not to have fancy diagrams, but for everyone on the team to be able to easily visualize the process. This is one benefit of the task mapping approach presented earlier in the book. Having a clear structure helps split the big problem into smaller ones, so it's easier to see what needs to be worked on. It will also make the impact of decisions more apparent, which helps open new pathways toward solving a given problem.

Not de-risking the technological approach

There's a butterfly effect in your robotic cell deployment: small early design choices have a big impact later in the project. To avoid any surprises, revisit the section on how to de-risk a concept. A small up-front investment in concept de-risking can prevent a big waste of time and money later on. Still, don't be afraid to revisit your assumptions. Your project is part innovation, which implies you won't know everything at the beginning and new information will be uncovered along the way.

It's possible that new equipment was chosen for the application that's simply not a good fit. Ideally you'll find this out in the de-risking phase. Unfortunately, sometimes you'll only realize it later in the project once new information has become available. Often people fall into the trap of the sunk-cost fallacy, rationalizing that "We've invested so much in this approach that we just have to keep investing until it works." And then you fight to make it work for weeks.

Instead of accepting that mistakes were made in choosing that equipment, returning the equipment, and going back to the design phase, people will waste even more time and effort on work-arounds here. But remember, it's not just about the cost of the equipment—you should also consider the cost of the output that's not being produced because the robotic cell is not in production on time.

The same argument applies to older machines. You wouldn't try connecting your iPhone to a 1988 Commodore 64 computer, but factories attempt essentially the same feat all the time. Integrating machines from different vendors and different eras that are not meant to communicate requires a lot of non-value-added work. Consider whether it might be better to change the other machine at the same time.

BAD PROGRAMMING PRACTICES

Not applying basic good programming practices can cause your team to waste a lot of time. The most common—and easily solvable—bad programming practices are described below.

BAD VERSIONING SYSTEM

Some teams jump into their programming without a standardized way to keep track of program versions. Very quickly, they get lost. They don't know whether rev_29 or rev_29(1) is the more recent file, so they have to stop programming while they figure it out. And when they do find out, they don't know what the difference is between the latest version and rev_28. This could all be avoided by naming versions according to a simple standard, such as rev_29.1 and rev_29.2, and letting everyone know how to do the same with their work.

Lack of program structure

Would you manufacture a product in your factory without having made a plan of it first? Not having a structure before diving into the code is like building a new machine with no plans and improvising new parts as you go. Just because it's software, doesn't mean you don't need to plan it!

Define the skeleton of your program. Break it down into smaller, logical blocks. You might do it on paper or sticky notes to begin with. It will be simpler to work on these blocks one at a time when you go back to the robot teach pendant.

Make sure you encapsulate logical blocks in functions with meaningful names to help people read and understand the program. If more than one person will be working on it, it's even more important to make sure that the different people can understand and contribute efficiently.

Abstract variable names

Vague variable names make it hard to read a program. For instance, it's much easier to understand "if ToolPosition_x > 200 then ..." than "if x > 200 then...". Define a plan for how you will get everyone to use meaningful names for variables.

Program not commented

Take the time to put comments in the program and keep them up to date. It will enable everyone to understand it faster.

Deficient testing procedures

When you develop new parts of the program or work to improve the existing program, the last thing you want to do is break things that used to be working. One way to avoid that is to have an efficient testing procedure.

This is especially important with robots, since mistakes in the program can cause damage to the system hardware when the tests are executed. I've seen dozens of robots smash their own tooling on a table during testing. Without proper testing, your robot might do the same—putting you at risk of taking two steps back for every one step forward.

NON-VALUE-ADDED ENGINEERING WORK

Which aspects of the engineering process—which starts with mapping the manual task—contribute towards having your robotic cell produce value, and which are merely a waste of time? We too often see resources wasted on non-value-added custom engineering work. It might be done to save a few hundred dollars or achieve a certain specification, but it can end up delaying your robotic cell startup date. Keep the end goal in mind. Look at the complete picture when evaluating price. Take into account the cost of the equipment, the custom engineering work itself, and the cost of having the robot starting production later.

Don't fall into the trap of continuously adding to the scope of the project as it goes along. Without noticing, you'll blow the budget and the schedule, destroying your ROI. To make sure you don't feel compelled to modify the MVRC until you complete it, the key is to have an efficient integrate phase.

For example, let's say you've defined your MVRC, which you've decided will include a gripper. But while engineering the gripper itself, you spend ages designing, fabricating, and testing customized versions of it. These things are important up to a certain point, but eventually they stop being necessary and start being a waste of time and effort. If you have a "maker's mindset," it's easy to get in a state of flow and tinker endlessly with your creation; but just because you can improve it even more, doesn't mean you should.

You should also pay attention to times when non-value-added tasks pile up one on top of the other. For example, if you have a non value-ue-added manual task being done because of a non-value-added robotic operation, don't add even more "non-value" by spending a lot of time engineering the parts for these tasks!

One area where this tends to happen is custom tooling for part presentation. Part presentation often involves non-value-added tasks that are done in order to overcome the robot's limitations, like manually filling custom fixtures. But if you over-engineer the fixture for part presentation, or spend too much time on tooling designs that can't ever be reused, you're simply compounding the amount of waste here.

The decisions you make about design and integration carry over into the operate phase. If you built a custom piece of tooling in the design phase, and this piece is critical to the cell's operation, you'll have to fabricate a spare one and store it in case the first one breaks. This extra inventory is waste... but if you don't have a spare, the resulting downtime will also be waste.

INEFFICIENT COMMUNICATION

Aside from the technical inefficiencies above, communication issues are the most common type of waste. Here are several reasons why.

A robotic cell is not self-contained

It needs to interface with machines from various suppliers. The machines may work perfectly on their own and come with good documentation. But they're usually not meant to work with each other. Since a lot of the difficult technical problems have to do with the interface between different machines, solving them entails coordinating people from different organizations. The more people are involved in a task, the more complex it becomes. People have different priorities, understandings of the problem, schedules, etc. This can result in a lot of waste from repeating the same information or waiting for new information to be delivered.

Robots deal with the real world

How do you describe a manual task to someone over the phone or through email? This type of information is clear when we can see and touch it. But it's hard to communicate it in a way that's both accurate and useful. Also, not everyone involved in the project necessarily knows what information is relevant to the deployment process. This often results in long, tedious exchanges of information.

For example, if an automation engineer asks a question to a supplier and the supplier can't answer it, the engineer must ask his colleagues additional questions just to get the information needed to answer the original question. The ideal scenario is for the engineer to gather all the relevant information before questioning the supplier. This is exactly what the manual task map aims to do for everyone. It systematizes the gathering of information, in order to make the exchange of information more efficient.

Robotic cell deployment is multidisciplinary

One of the most fun aspects of robotics is how it combines various types of expertise. This is also one of the most challenging. You need people with different perspectives and different tools to work together to achieve a common goal.

As soon as you have more than one person working on a project, you need a way to get everyone on the same page. One method is a task board (such as a dry-erase whiteboard) where you write down the steps of your automation project and check them off as they're achieved. Another way is to host agile development-inspired "scrum meetings"—short, daily meetings where everyone shares what they've done since the last meeting, what they will do before the next, and whether they're facing any delays.

In all cases, make sure there's a clear definition of people's roles, responsibilities, and the chain of approval. For example, the mechanical engineer who's working on the part presentation jig should know what the robot's programmer is expecting in terms of adequate part presentation. Since the most common type of communication waste is delays in getting the right information, you should strive to ensure all transmitted information is complete, accurate, timely, and sent to the right people.

MULTITASKING

To be productive in any creative, technical work—such as designing and integrating robotic cells—you need to focus. We often see factories where the automation engineer responsible for the *proactive* robotic cell project is also on the front line for urgent *reactive* internal support calls. Every time there's an issue with another machine in production, the engineer has to stop working on the robotic cell deployment and go fix it. When he returns to the cell, it takes time to get into a productive state of mind again. Then some progress can be made... until another "emergency" arises.

Next thing you know, the robotic cell project is six weeks behind schedule. And if you started your ROI calculation where I advised doing so (from when you started the design phase, not from when the cell starts producing), the payback on your investment will take a major hit.

Many successful manufacturers overcome this challenge by hiring a new employee to take charge of the robotic deployment. Since the new hire hasn't worked on any past projects at the company, her colleagues won't come to her saying "Can you please debug that machine you installed last year?" She'll be able to focus on developing her core robotics expertise, which is what will move this and future cell deployment projects forward.

SUMMARY

Table 17: Potential sources of waste in the design phase.

Design Phase	
Type of waste	**Examples**
Transportation	› Site visit from suppliers › Walking around the factory › Components delivery
Waiting	› Waiting for people to be available, for answers, or for components to arrive › Long meetings where nothing is decided › Waiting to have enough time to actually work on the project
Overproduction	› Over-designing, rather than sticking to the MVRC
Defects	› Making errors in the design that will result in a non-functioning or unreliable robotic cell › Accidentally ordering the wrong parts
Inventory	› Waiting for components to be designed and produced
Motion	› Finding a place to do the project in-house, moving stuff around
Extra processing	› Custom engineering, purchasing, logistics work, inefficient communication
Underutilizing human potential	› Multi-tasking, wasting time going from one project to another › Having highly skilled people doing tedious, low-level, yet necessary technical work

Mura	› Waiting until robotic cells are urgently needed, which results in non-ideal decisions being made to save time
	› Interrupting work to respond to emergencies outside the design project
Muri	› Assigning overly busy engineers to robotic cell deployment tasks
	› Assigning projects that are too complex for team members to handle

Table 18: Potential sources of waste in the integrate phase

Integrate Phase	
Type of waste	**Examples**
Transportation	› On-site support › Sending components back and forth › Bringing necessary tools to and from the workspace each day
Waiting	› Waiting for answers › Waiting for components to arrive › Waiting in meetings › Waiting to have time to actually work on the project
Overproduction	› Installing the robot before the rest of the production line is ready for it (this one is rare)
Defects	› Integration errors that must be redone › Damaging parts during integration
Inventory	› Assigning more people, material, or investment money to the project than is necessary › Storing components for a long time because you're not ready to use them yet
Motion	› Multitasking, going from one project to another

Extra processing	› High administrative overhead due to unnecessary paperwork
Underutilizing human potential	› Having highly skilled people doing repetitive debugging and installation work
Mura	› Interrupting work to respond to emergencies outside the integration project
Muri	› Assigning overly busy engineers to robotic cell deployment tasks › Assigning projects that are too complex for team members to handle

PREPARE TO SCALE

In most cases, your lean robotics journey will not end with the deployment of your first robot. Once you've completed your first design-integrate-operate cycle, you'll likely start seeing new ways to keep improving productivity with robots.

If you intend to harness the power of robots throughout your factory(ies), this section is for you.

Remember how we distinguished between what creates value and what doesn't when deploying a robotic cell? If you want to scale, you'll want to organize your work to:

- Get rid of non-value-added activities.
- Perform value-added activities faster and better.

The keys to doing so are **standardizing** the various aspects of your cell deployment, and **building robotics skills** among your team members.

STANDARDIZE

If you want to scale, standardization will bring many benefits that translate directly into a higher return on your robotic cell investment.

You can standardize many aspects of your cell deployment, including methodology, hardware, and programming.

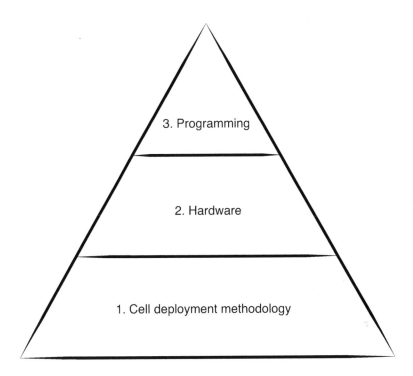

Fig. 44: The standardization pyramid. Numbers indicate the order in which standardization should be attempted.

The deployment methodology is the easiest thing to standardize, so you should do that first. Next comes the hardware. It's not always possible to standardize hardware, but if you manage to do so, you can then try standardizing your programming. The standardization order is shown in Fig. 44.

I recommend that you put more emphasis on the standardization of hardware and programming once you have completed your first deployment. At that point, will have a better idea of the potential for efficiency gains. You will also have a better sense of where robots will be applicable in your factory. If you do aim to deploy many cells in the future, investing the time and effort needed to standardize at that point will pay off in the form of faster, easier, and smoother future deployments. It will also make the maintenance and optimization of the robotic cell fleet much more efficient.

HERE ARE FIVE REASONS WHY YOU SHOULD STANDARDIZE:

1. Efficiencies during the design and integrate phases

By standardizing your methods and tools, you'll be able to reuse them for different projects. At every new project no time will be wasted on searching for the right tools and methods, so you can start doing valuable work right away.

2. More uptime (less downtime) in the operate phase

Using standard components also pays off during the operate phase. It's more efficient to maintain a fleet of similar cells than to maintain the same number of cells that were each made with custom parts. With custom parts, you'll have to keep inventories of spare parts, or face long delays when they inevitably break.

3.Efficiencies in communication

When you use the same methods and the same vocabulary to describe aspects of the robotic cell, it helps ensure your team members have the same background knowledge, which lets them understand each other's perspectives on a situation.

4. Higher returns on your innovation investment

Standard methods and tools make it easier to train and coach people, because you can capture details of the standardized deployment process in documents that are used for training.

5. Higher returns on your capital investment

Ultimately, the four reasons above will translate into deploying more productive robotic cells, more quickly—thus generating a bigger return, sooner.

STANDARDIZE YOUR DEPLOYMENT PROCESS

The goal of this book is to give you a standard framework for your robotic cell deployment projects. The framework will help you define your target and the steps to reaching it. After a few projects, it will also help you identify the team's robotic cell deployment capacity, meaning the number of robotic cells that they can deploy and manage.

As you learn from past experiences, you'll be able to point out precise areas where you need to improve. The framework will help you compare potential projects in terms of their benefits and complexity. It will also help you communicate the project's goals with your team, others at your company, and external suppliers. Eventually, everyone involved in robotic cell deployment will become familiar with the project's phases.

You probably already have some templates, such as for breaking down project steps or calculating ROI, that your company uses to speed up business processes. Now's the time to add lean robotics templates, which you can find at leanrobotics.org, to this manufacturing management toolbox.

STANDARDIZE YOUR HARDWARE

Can any of your robotic cell components be reused from one cell to another? An obvious one is the type of robot. Although robots are getting simpler to use, the cost of switching is still quite high due to the need to retrain employees.

When choosing your robotic arm provider, you'll of course consider the cost, reliability, and support level—but if you have scaling in mind, you should also consider the following factors:

- **Application range inside your factory(ies)**
  Whether the robot is suited to your application depends on its specifications, such as reach, payload, speed, and repeatability. It also depends on how well the robot works with the tooling and surrounding machines that you need for your processes.

- **Ease of training your staff**
  Your people are the key to keeping your factory floor adaptable, so you want to choose a robot that's easy for many workers to use. This will minimize the risk of having only a few people who know how to operate it. It will enable more people to ensure the robotic cells stay productive in the future. While they keep the current cells running, your technical champions can work on greater value-added tasks like design and integration of new cells.

- **Efficiency of cell design, integration, and operation**
  Which brand of robot offers you the opportunity to minimize waste throughout the entire deployment cycle? Which allows you to measure the amount of value it's creating for the next station?

Other examples of reusable hardware building blocks are the end-of-arm tooling, sensors, and stands, as well as devices for cable management, safety, and part presentation. Don't just look at the hardware's capacity—you also need to think about how it can be integrated with the robot.

Remember that even if each item works great on its own, the hard part is putting them together. When considering which ones to buy, ask suppliers to demonstrate how their product can be installed, configured, and (if relevant) programmed. You should ask the same questions about these items that you asked when choosing a robot: are they flexible enough to cover a wide range of applications? Are they easy to understand, install, program, and maintain?

Aside from these benefits, standardizing your hardware is also necessary for standardizing your programming, which will bring further efficiencies. Since there is currently no standard way for a robot to communicate with external tools and other devices, any robot program you write will be highly dependent on specific hardware your cell is using. If the hardware changes from one cell to the other, you won't be able to reuse the software "building blocks" that you developed for previous cells—you'll have to write new ones just to accomplish the same thing. This is yet another reason why you should standardize your hardware.

STANDARDIZE YOUR PROGRAMMING

As factories become more digitized, computer-controlled machines are turning the traditional factory floor into a software enterprise. Even if you're the only one programming a single robot, you'll be more efficient if you standardize how you program. A defined standard helps when you need to troubleshoot after not having worked on the cell for some time. And as soon as you have more than one person programming the robots, it's a no-brainer. Having a common way to program will help everyone work more efficiently, and it will be much easier to add new programmers to the team later.

Standardized programming will also pay off when you have more than one robot. You don't want to reinvent the wheel for each new application; you want to reuse your work as much as possible to finish the deployment faster.

In any robotic cell project, certain basic standards are always worth implementing:

- **Programming standards**
  - › For structuring the program
  - › For naming variables
  - › For commenting on the code

- **Testing procedures**
  - › For testing a modified program before putting it into production

By contrast, the following programming standards only make sense to implement if you already have standardized hardware building blocks in place first:

- **Standard functions**
  - › Encapsulating sets of frequently used instructions in reusable robot functions (including data exchange with external components or machines)
  - › Keeping the functions up-to-date
  - › Saving the reusable functions—perhaps in a central repository of programs and functions that you can choose from when programming a new application

- **Robotic cell configuration**
  - › Configuring multiple robotic cells in the same way, such as by using the same I/Os (data-transferring programs, operations, or devices) in each cell

- **Application templates**
  - › Developing templates that can serve as starting points for programming the most frequently needed applications

- **Development tools**
    - › Using a standard programming environment and/
      or simulators
    - › If you use a simulator, using a simulation library

Lean robotics in action: How Procter & Gamble standardized to deploy robotic cells globally

P&G is a multinational manufacturer of product ranges including family, personal and household care products. Many of their factories and distribution centers have similar applications. Still, there are various local differences in the products made, packaging, and technical know-how of their team members. When scaling up their robotic cell deployment efforts, P&G invested in understanding how certain standard approaches could be used globally. By finding the right balance between standard building blocks, standard cells, and the possibility to adapt them locally, P&G has managed to deploy over 100 robotic cells in the past two years.[1]

BUILD YOUR SKILLS

Leveraging your skills is a core lean robotics principle. In fact, it is crucial to the success of your robotics deployment. The companies that we've seen reap the most sustainable long-term rewards from robots are the ones who've invested in developing their robotics skills

---

(1) Barrett Brunsman, "P&G relying more on robots to cut costs," Cincinnati Business Courier, September 13, 2016, https://www.bizjournals.com/cincinnati/news/2016/09/13/p-g-rely-ing-more-on-robots-to-cut-costs.html.

starting at the beginning of their very first project.

WHY YOU SHOULD BUILD THE LEAN ROBOTICS SKILLSET

Isn't it important to build all skills on the manufacturing floor, not just the robotics-related ones? Yes; in a perfect world, everyone would be trained in everything that could have a positive effect on their work. But none of us have infinite time or resources for training, so we need to make a choice.

Here's why robotics skills should be high on your business's list of priorities.

Robotics can have a broad impact across the factory.

Robots are like computers: general machines that can execute various processes. You have computers on the desks of your engineers, executives, accountants and shipping personnel. In a similar way, you'll eventually see robots in the packing/unpacking, assembly, quality control, and logistics areas. Your investment in robotics skills has the potential to pay off throughout the factory by making numerous functions more efficient.

Robotics skills are necessary for maximizing your robot ROI

If you're able to deploy robotic cells efficiently with your own in-house team, this will drastically lower the cost of cell deployment, maintenance, and upgrading. If you have a few skilled employees, you'll be able to delegate your projects to external system integrators—and since your team includes a few people who understand the technology, your project will be much better managed. However, if you and your team have no robotics skills at all, you'll be highly dependent on external resources and you'll be at risk of going with decisions that aren't in your best interests.

Limited robotics skills put your business at risk

If only one key employee knows how to operate robots, then you've just created a single point of failure in your system. So it's just as important to invest in a resilient, knowledgeable team as it is to invest in the robotics equipment itself.

SKILLS TO DEVELOP

So what are the robotics deployment skills that you need to develop internally? Table 19 summarizes them. As you'll see, each skill aligns with a phase of robotic cell deployment.

Table 19: Summary of the lean robotics skills to develop. Grey rows indicate technology-dependent skills.

PROJECT MANAGEMENT SKILLS	With this skill you can:
Robotic cell deployment project management	• Define a robotic cell deployment project. • Assemble and mobilize the team to execute the project successfully.
DESIGN SKILLS	**With this skill you can:**
Manual task mapping	• Document how a manual process is currently done with the information that will be needed to design the robotic cell.
Robotic cell concept	Develop a high-level robotic cell concept, including: • Layout • Choice of components • Operation sequence (outfeed, infeed, process)
Robotic task mapping	• Document how a given process will be done with a robotic cell.

Manual-robotic comparison	• Compare the manual cell map with the robotic cell map. • Identify the modifications that will be needed upstream and downstream of the cell. • Identify modifications in information transmission when going from a manual to robotic cell.
Robotic cell design	Carry out the robotic cell engineering work, including: • Mechanical drawings (custom tooling, enclosures, part infeed, outfeed, etc.) • Electrical plans • Control architecture • Prototyping, proof-of-concepts
Robotic cell safety	• Execute a safety risk assessment. • Develop strategies to reduce the risk to an appropriate level.
INTEGRATE SKILLS	**With this skill you can:**
Mechanical installation	• Assemble the robotic cell components as per the design instructions.
Electrical installation	• Assemble the robotic cell components as per the design instructions.
Industrial communication	• Interface different machines and sensors so they can communicate with each other.
Programming	• Develop a high-level logic sequence. • Write the robotic cell's program.
Process	• Adapt a manual process so it can be done by a robot.
OPERATE SKILLS	**With this skill you can:**
Maintenance and troubleshooting	• Identify the source of the robotic cell's problem and resolve it. • Maintain a robotic cell in good working condition.

In the table above, the items in rows with white backgrounds are general skills—they don't depend on a specific vendor or piece of technology. Meanwhile, the items in rows with grey backgrounds are more particular to the specific technology or vendor equipment you're working on. For example, just because you can program one brand of robot, doesn't mean you can program another brand of robot. Some concepts will be similar, but there will also be plenty of instructions in the robot languages that differ from one to another.

Which skills should you and your team members focus on acquiring? To answer this question, start by assessing the current skill level in your organization. Answer these questions for each item in the table above:

- Who in your organization has this skill?
- How critical is this skill?
    - If you were to lose the team member(s) with this skill, how detrimental would the effect be on your cell deployment (especially in terms of cost and productivity)?
    - If a team member gained this skill, how positive would the effect be on your cell deployment?

A template is available on leanrobotics.org.

Regardless of how you rank the skills, you shouldn't start deploying robots without basic skills for handling the beginning (manual task mapping) and end (troubleshooting, maintenance) of the deployment cycle.

Manual task mapping is a useful tool for evaluating your potential robotization projects. If you work with external system integrators, documenting the process with a manual task map will help you communicate efficiently. Once you've completed a few mapping exercises and the relevant concept work (either in-house or with the help of external resources) your team will have a better sense of what is easy, possible, and impossible to achieve with robots.

The troubleshooting and maintenance skills will help ensure you're able to keep the robotic cell running once it's in production.

In the middle of the deployment cycle are the more "hardcore robotics" skills, which include design, engineering, and programming. Developing these skills from the ground up will require a large investment, but it is absolutely doable and can bring a large payoff. In fact, these skills make up the bulk of the cost when a system integrator does a project for you. Developing those skills will enable you to deploy robotic cells internally, and just as importantly, modify your early robotic cells to keep pace as your manufacturing needs evolve.

HOW TO DEVELOP YOUR TEAM'S SKILLS

To develop those skills, you'll hire new employees or train existing ones—or both.

If you're starting from scratch and your automation engineering team is already stretched thin over many projects, look to hire an experienced engineer with the hardcore robotics skills. Find someone who can understand the nitty-gritty aspects of the project while seeing the big picture—someone with great communication and teaching skills for sharing knowledge with the existing team and future hires.

Keep in mind that many of the skills that you're trying to find in this person will be dependent on a specific vendor or technology. Make sure the candidate can apply these skills to new technologies and that she's willing to work with new vendors, not just her old favorites. The technologies she used in the past might not be the exact ones that you need, so find someone who's open-minded about robotic solutions.

If your existing team has the time and ability to focus, and a basic technical background, then they're able to learn robotics skills. The best way to learn is by doing, so have your team pick up skills while they work on projects. Start with simple deployments, and allow enough time in the schedule for the initial slow progress along the learning curve. Doing projects in collaboration with external system integrators is a great way to build skills while getting concrete short-term results. With every project done this way, remember to define the specific skills you're aiming to have your team develop.

As you saw in Table 19, many skills are technology- or vendor-dependent. This is one reason why standardizing can accelerate your skills development. By focusing on a given set of technologies, you can increase the depth of your team's skills, as opposed to merely broadening their ability to do basic things with many different technologies. Increasing the depth of skills with one standard technology will expand the range of applications that can be automated in your factory and improve the performance and robustness of your cells. Plus, the more team members you have who understand a similar technology, the more opportunities there are to have them coach and support each other.

SUCCEEDING WITH LEAN ROBOTICS

The previous parts of the book explained why you should implement lean robotics, how to do it while deploying a robotic cell, and how you can reduce waste to scale your efforts company-wide. This final section is about management lessons from the field: how to use the methodology while managing robotics projects to maximize your chances of success.

WHERE TO FOCUS: IMPORTANT VS. URGENT

When you're too busy to invest in working smarter, you keep being too busy *because* you didn't invest in working smarter. It's a vicious cycle that I call the "reactivity spiral." When you're trapped in the spiral, you can't allocate any time for the things that are important but not immediately urgent until they *are* urgent... and by then it's too late.

Deploying robots on your factory floor is often one of those "important but not immediately urgent" tasks. Will you act now, or wait for "non-urgency" to become "emergency"?

Generally speaking, if you're always in reactivity mode and never building the future of your company, you're failing in your duties as a manufacturing manager or engineer. It is your responsibility to allocate enough resources to invest in operating more efficiently in the future. You can complain that you're understaffed and keep doing the same thing day in, day out. Or you can take responsibility, find solutions, and take charge of projects that will change your business for the better and make it more sustainable.

Yes, technology is getting better every day. But the demand for workers who are skilled in robotics is also increasing every day, as is the productivity of factories that have already deployed robots successfully. So you need to find a way for you and your team to break the reactivity spiral.

Deploying robots might seem risky when you look at it before your first project. But continuing to do nothing can be even riskier. In a manufacturing world that's moving ever faster, standing still is the biggest risk you can take for your company and your career.

WHAT TO DO IN PRACTICE

1. If you've decided robotics can have a broad positive impact on your company, bring your evidence to senior management and push for robotics to become part of the company's strategy.
2. Once management accepts robotics as an important initiative, ensure the necessary resources are allocated to the project.
3. Set clear short-term goals (quarterly, monthly, weekly), communicate them to your team, and track performance.

START SIMPLE

In many of the factories I've visited, the management and engineering teams are on board with robotics and eager to get going, but they don't know where to start. Although the answer is to start simple, this begs the question: "What is simple?" The tools presented in this book will help you answer this question for your context.

- **Task mapping**

  In the design phase of the robotic cell deployment, we explained how to map the manual process, make an equivalent map for the robotic concept, and then compare the two in the manual-to-robotic comparison. With this analysis, you can identify exactly what will need to change to go from the manual process to a robotic one.

- **Assessing your internal skills**

  In the section about building your internal skills, we listed the skills you, or people on your team, need to have. With the skills you already have, can you complete the project you've mapped, or are some important parts missing?

By combining the task mapping for a cell with your understanding of your available skills, you can determine whether your project will be simple or complex.

Then you'll want to compare this complexity with the potential return on your investment. With the complexity level and the potential ROI, you can compare different projects along a complexity-benefits quadrant like the one shown in Fig. 45.

Note that the projects on the chart, and their potential ROI, will be particular to your company: what's complicated for you might be easy for another company. For instance, it's simple for employees of a machine shop to design and build part presentation trays, but it might be more difficult for them to interface machines together. The opposite might be true for companies with broader software expertise and limited mechanical know-how.

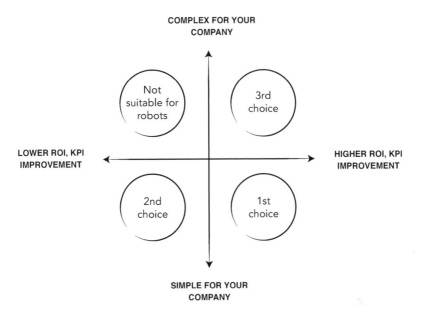

Fig. 45: Complexity-benefits quadrant.

You should start with projects in the bottom half of the chart. The ideal case is a simple application with a high ROI, of course. But if you need to choose between a simple, low-ROI application and a complex, high-ROI one, it's best to go with the simple one. This is one area where we diverge from traditional lean manufacturing, which advises focusing on the next high-ROI continuous improvement project.

The bigger the first project is, the more uncertain your forecasts will be, for both the project plan and the ROI. Far better to start simple, and make sure the first cell deployment is a success, so you can start creating value with it while building momentum for more ambitious future projects.

However simple your chosen project is, you also need to check that it matches your employees' skill level. Psychology research shows that this is one important factor for both individuals and teams to enjoy work and be most productive.[1] If the task is too hard, your team will feel stuck and discouraged; what you want is a challenge that will stretch your team's skills and inspire them to learn.

WHAT TO DO IN PRACTICE

1. When choosing among potential first projects, place them on the complexity-benefits quadrant.
2. Choose your first project from the simple sections, not the complex ones.

KEEP IT SIMPLE

Not only should you start simple, but you should also keep it simple along the way. During the design and integrate phases, it might be tempting to modify the scope of the robotic cell. Some new nice-to-have's will inevitably appear. Resist the temptation to add them as they come. If you do, you'll soon realize that complexity has crept in, that you are over schedule and over budget. By combining longer delays before production with a higher cost, you ROI will drop significantly. Just as importantly, the project will become a magnet for team members' dissatisfactions and robotics will lose credibility in your company.

You might ask: "What if I realize I missed something critical (not a nice-to-have) at the design phase, and I'm already in the integration phase?" It is possible that you'll indeed have to change your MVRC plans. However, the whole process is structured to prevent this from happening.

---

(1) See Mihaly Csikszentmihalyi, *Flow: The Psychology of Optimal Experience*, Harper Perennial Modern Classics, 2008. First published 1990.

WHAT TO DO IN PRACTICE

1. Always remember that a cell produces zero value until it's successfully in the operate stage.
2. Start simple—and if you've lost your way, re-start simple!
3. De-risk the most critical parts of the robotic cell concept.
4. Define a clear MVRC and make sure your team agrees on it.
5. Avoid changing the MVRC until after the cell has started producing value.

BE REALISTIC

Is your team already stretched too thin over dozens of projects? Do you have trouble completing current projects? Does every day at work involve a new emergency for you to deal with? And yet, you want to add a robotics project on top of all that (without any additional resources)? Please, be realistic.

Deploying robots will require your team to focus. Set them up for success. Assign a technical lead that has the time and ability to make it work. Also keep in mind that many people in the team will have to be coordinated, especially in the integrate phase. There will be modifications to the production line that will affect many people, so these workers also need to have time to spare.

Aside from resources, you should also be realistic about the project's outcome. Robots are transformative technologies for your manufacturing floor, but they're not magical. They require work and persistence to reap benefits on a large scale. Be aware that teams will typically go through the change in opinions shown in Fig. 46.

When you first get the idea for a robotic cell ("Let's get a robot!"), you'll be full of excitement. As you watch videos of robots doing amazing things, you might think "Wow, this will solve all our problems!" Then you'll come crashing down a bit when you officially begin the deployment and realize robots aren't a miraculous cure-all. But as you work through the learning curve, you'll eventually have a productive robot.

Knowing about this cycle of opinions in advance will help you keep things in perspective. You'll avoid being both over-optimistic at the beginning, and overly freaked-out when you face the challenges of implementation. Hopefully the tools provided in this book will break down the problems into smaller, clearer, easier ones so you can sail right through the "Might be more complicated..." phase.

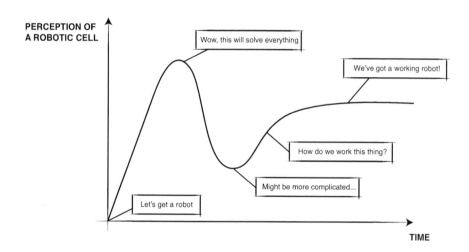

Fig. 46: The typical change in opinions about a robotic cell during a deployment project.

WHAT TO DO IN PRACTICE

1. Allocate sufficient resources to the project, while being realistic about the amount of focus and time your employees can dedicate to it.
2. Expect the unexpected regarding your implementation, since you'll be learning while you work through it.

SHARE KNOWLEDGE

You can have your team read this book, watch dozens of applications videos, and go through online case studies... these are all great sources of inspiration. However, when consuming content online, you can always wonder if it's marketing material. When hearing about other companies' triumphs, you can always question if their cases are too different from your own context to be relevant.

The most inspiring teachers will be their peers. People are all ears when one of their colleagues explains how, in practice, he has successfully deployed a robot. Setting up a question-and-answer meeting like this can prompt lively discussions, as people ask precise questions that are tied into their reality, their company's culture, financials, products, processes, etc. You should create opportunities for this knowledge sharing to happen. This is a great way to celebrate success and recognize your team's hard work. Sharing best practices and standard development tools is also a great way to leverage your investment in innovation and scale your robotics deployment efforts throughout your factory(ies).

WHAT TO DO IN PRACTICE

1. Document your projects with snapshots of the "before and after" and the impact on KPIs. ("Snapshots" is meant both literally, i.e. pictures/videos, and metaphorically, i.e. data.)
2. Identify credible "robotics evangelists" in the team who can inspire other people in your company.
3. Proactively create opportunities for knowledge sharing such as documenting and sharing internal case studies or organizing seminars.

WHY NOW IS THE TIME FOR LEAN ROBOTICS

As Marc Andreessen, venture capitalist and former Netscape executive, famously pronounced, "software is eating the world."[1] When you're buying a car today, a significant chunk of what you're paying for is the software used in the vehicle. When you're watching a movie, a good portion of the work was done with software, whether it was for special effects, editing, or just the equipment used for filming. This is happening for every part of the economy, including in your factory.

Yes, you may be transforming physical materials and selling physical products. But increasingly, the jobs in your factory will look more like IT jobs than welding jobs. Machines now are all controlled by computers, not only by mechanical or electrical means like in the past, and they're getting more and more connected. So manufacturing workers are increasingly having to gain software and IT skills.

Think it's hard to find a manual worker today? Have you started recruiting people with robotics skills? If you haven't already, you'll quickly realize it can be even harder, especially if you are in a remote area. Whereas before you may have been competing for workers with the factory down the street, now you're going up against companies in all industries, including tech giants like Google, Uber, and Amazon, all of which are hiring robotics graduates. The demand for robotics skills will only increase as robots are adopted more broadly in all industries.

The longer you wait to build your own in-house expertise, the harder it

---

(1) Marc Andreessen, "Why Software Is Eating The World," Wall Street Journal, August 20, 2011, https://www.wsj.com/articles/SB100014240531119034809045765122509156 29460.

gets—and the further behind you'll lag in productivity, relative to your competitors. Even if you hire an external system integrator to do most of the work, you'll still need a way to specify and follow-up on the projects. If you don't have the means to rehire those integrators every time, you and your team had better be able to do those things yourselves.

Some might complain that young people today are being too picky, not wanting to get their hands dirty and get the tough jobs done. I believe that they're rightly striving to do more with their lives, to not only work harder but smarter. The good news is, you need more tech skills to complement your manufacturing skills and that's exactly what they have to offer.

Lean robotics can help you build the new manufacturing skillset.

- Using the people before robots principle will help you prioritize robotic technologies that are accessible to more people. Your manufacturing team members will be able to build their robotics skills.
- Adding the principle of leveraging your skills, you will reduce risk of having crucial know-how locked in the heads of just a few people in your factory.
- You'll continuously groom internal skills at your company, reducing its dependency on increasingly scarce external resources.

Lean robotics is possible today because of recent technological advances. It is necessary today because of all the challenges that manufacturers are facing. Innovative manufacturers will see this convergence as a unique opportunity. They will leverage robots to do more with less and become more successful companies. Will you be among those who can make robots work in their factories? I wish you great success!

GLOSSARY

Term	Definition
Andon	"Signal" in Japanese. The andon is activated when something in the station is not working properly, and serves as a visual cue to draw the worker's attention.
Cell layout	A geometric representation of the components of a cell.
Customer	Any person, machine, department, or company that receives the output of a process. The customer can be internal to a factory (e.g., the next cell in a production line) or external (e.g., the person who buys what the factory makes). The end user of a product is called the "consumer".
Error-proofing	Also known as "poka-yoke" (the Japanese term), this is the practice of putting mechanisms in place to prevent machines or operators from inadvertently making mistakes.

Term	Definition
Gemba	"The real place" in Japanese. When you go to the gemba, you go to where the value is created—which in lean robotics means going to the actual manufacturing station where a robot is (or will be) deployed.
Manual task map	A document that describes how a manual task is currently done. Includes information on the manual task process and on how value is created for the cell's customer. It also includes information that will be useful when coming up with a robotic cell concept.
Minimum viable robotic cell (MVRC)	A concept of the simplest, most cost-effective robotic cell that will provide the value its customer needs.
Monument	A piece of equipment that cannot easily (or cost-effectively) be adapted or moved in response to changes in manufacturing needs.
Robotic cell deployment cycle	The sequence of how you get a robotic cell to work in your factory. Consists of three phases: design, integrate and operate. The design and integrate phases are about planning and installing the robotic cell. The operate phase is about having a robotic cell that continuously produces value.

Term	Definition
Robotic task map	A document that describes how a robotic task will be done. Includes information on the robotic cell process and how the robotic cell will provide value for its customer.
Value-added	Describes any activity that meets these three criteria: 1. It must transform the product or service. 2. The customer must be willing to "pay" for it. 3. It must be done correctly the first time.
Value stream mapping	A lean manufacturing method that captures information about how the various steps in a process create value for the customer.
Waste	There are three types of waste: Muda—Anything that does not add value for the customer. (In lean robotics, there are eight types of muda.) Mura—Waste caused by variation. Muri—Waste caused by overburdening equipment or people.

53792967R00125

Made in the USA
San Bernardino, CA
28 September 2017